Step-by-Step
Knifemaking

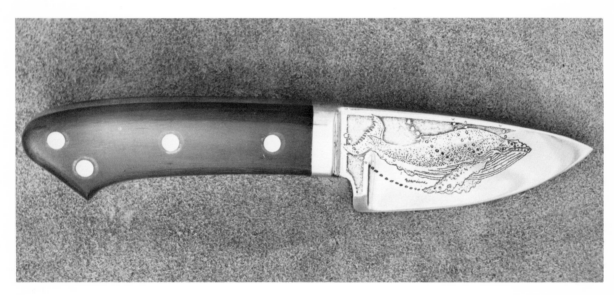

A 2½-inch dropped-edge utility skinner with buffalo horn handle.
Humpback Whale etching by Francine Martin.

Step-by-Step
Knifemaking
You Can Do It!

by David Boye

Drawings by Robert J. Caradonna
Photos by Grant Heidrich
David Boye
Franklin Avery

 **Rodale Press** Emmaus, PA

Library of Congress Cataloging in Publication Data

Boye, David.
    Step-by-step knifemaking.

    Includes index.
    1. Metal-work. Knives.   I. Title.
TT213.B69   621.9′3   77-22382
ISBN O-87857-180-9
ISBN O-87857-181-7 pbk.

Printed in the United States of America.

2 4 6 8 10 9 7 5 3 1

This book is dedicated to
Sri Darwin Gross,
who helps on the inside.

Contents

Foreword XI

Preface XIII

Introduction XV

1. Starting Out 1
   The First Knife 1
   What Is a Good Knife? 6
      Design • Workmanship • Materials • User's
      versus Collector's Knives
   A Knifemaker's Overview 9
      Basic Skills • What Is a Good Blade? • What Kind
      of Steel? • Saw-blade Steel • Analysis of Saw-
      blade Steel • Corrosion

2. Tools 19
   Oxyacetylene Torch 20
   Motors and Power Application 21
      Variable Speed Machines
   Electric Power 23
      Phase • Voltage • Amperage • Wiring
   High-speed Grinders 25
      Grinding Wheel Safety • Grinding Arbor •
      Proper Direction for the Tightening Threads •
      The Work Rest • Pressure Guide for Production
      Grinding • Grinding Wheels
   Belt Sander/Grinders 28
      Controlling the Belt • Clearance • Abrasive Belts
      • The Platen or Work Wheel • Work Rest •
      Sleeve-type Drum Sanders • Abrasive Strip
      Drum Sanders • The "Flap-sander"
   Other Equipment 33
      Drill Press • Band Saw • Electric Kiln • Forge •
      Anvil • Micrometer • Small Tools
   Arranging the Shop 37
      Lighting

3. Different Kinds of Knives 41
      Vegetable Knife • Filet Knives • The Butcher
      Knife • Carving Knife • Carving Fork • Boning
      Knife • Chopping Knives • Bread Knives • Paring
      Knives • Meat Cleavers • Skinning Knives •
      Utility Knife • Hatchet
   Different Types of Handles 56
   Designing the Knife 58
      Designing the Handle

4. Cutting Out the Blade **61**

Drawing the Knife onto the Steel 61
  Cutting the Steel with a Torch • Cutting the
  Steel with a Band Saw
Refining the Shape 65
  Straightening the Blade

5. Grinding the Blade **69**

Types of Ground Edges 69
  The Proper Attitude • Grinding Technique • The
  Hollow Grind • The Straight Bevel • The Convex
  Bevel or Rolled Edge
Finger Guard for Dropped Blade 74
How Much to Grind Before Heat-treating 75
  Preparing the Blade for Heat-treating •
  Regrinding the Blade

6. Building the Bolster, Finger Guard, and Butt Plate **79**

Brazing on the Bolster and/or Butt Cap 81
  What Kind of Brass?
Bolster Construction for a Full-tang Slab Handle 82
  Brazing Technique • Brazing the Butt Piece •
  Fairing Down the Bolster • Removing a Hole
Building a Bolster for a Partial-tang One-piece Handle 97
Silver-soldering the Bolster and Butt Cap 100
  Ready-made Bolster/Finger Guards
Connecting the Bolster with Pins 102

7. Heat-treating the Carbon Steel Blade **105**

Hardening the Blade 105
  Warpage • Discoloration • Decarburization •
  Internal Decay • Hardness, Toughness, and
  Wear Resistance • Grain Growth • Quenching
  Temperature • The Quenching Bath
Tempering the Blade 116
  Tempering Colors
Annealing the Backbone and Handle Areas 117
  Annealing Underneath the Bolster • Spark Test
  for Hardness • How Hard Is Hard?

8. Trueing Up the Blade **123**

  Hammering the Blade • Untwisting the Blade •
  Wavy Edge • Straightening at the Bolster

9. Regrinding and Polishing the Blade **129**
  Removing the Grinder Marks • A Short Cut

10. Drilling Rivet Holes 137
  Placement of the Holes • Changing the Place-
  ment of a Metal Rivet Hole • Losing Weight •
  Drill Bits • Sharpening a Drill Bit • Use Tooling
  Fluid

11. Rivets and Pins, Pins and Rivets 143
  Brass Pins 143
  Inexpensive Rivets 145
  Improving the Rivets • Making a Countersink
  Bit • How to Set the Brake-shoe Rivets •
  Removing a Rivet
  Knifemaker's Rivets 149

12. Handle Materials 151
  Wood 151
  Milling the Wood
  Handles from Animals 152
  Micarta 153
  Moisture and Stability 153
  A Drying Kiln

13. Making a Full-tang Scale Handle 157
  Cutting Out the Slabs 157
  Fitting the Scales to the Tang • Fitting the Scales
  to the Bolster • Drilling the Holes in the Slabs
  Clamping the Scales to the Shank 163
  Epoxy Glue • Fastening the Scales to the Shank
  Shaping the Handle 168
  Getting into the Tight Spots • Making Finger
  Grips • Which Grit Sizes? • Finishing the Back of
  the Blade and the Bolster • Wood Filler • Heal-
  ing Wood Checks and Hairline Cracks • "Flap-
  sanding" the Handle • Danish Oil

14. The Partial-tang One-piece Handle 177
  Finishing the Handle

15. Buffing the Knife 183
  Buffing Safety • Cleaning the Buffing Wheel

16. Sharpening and Maintenance 189
  Forming the Burr • Stropping the Edge with the
  Buffer • How to "See" the Sharpness
  Hand-sharpening 192
  Tools • Cleaning the Whetstone • Sharpening •
  Stropping the Blade
  Maintenance of the Knife 197

17. Step-by-Step Checklist 199
    Step-by-Step Order of Process for Full-tang Handle
    with Brass Bolster 199

18. Production Notes 203
        Mass versus Individual Production • Developing
        a Relationship with Your Tools • The Strategy •
        Regrinding After Tempering • Water-cooled Belt
        Grinder • Oil-cooled Belt Grinder • Building a
        Stock of Blades

19. Etching Designs into the Steel 211
    Preparing the Surface of the Blade 211
        Applying the Wax • The Etching Tool • Cutting
        the Artwork into the Wax
    Using the Acid Bath 214
        Mixing the Acid • The Temperature of the Acid
        Bath • Light • The Bath • Biting the Knife
    Multilayer Etching 225
    Artwork 225

20. Sheathmaking 233
        Making a Snap Sheath • Making a Pouch Sheath

Appendix: Introduction to Alloy Steels 249
    The Anatomy and Physiology of Alloy Steel 250
    Adding Alloys 251
        Carbon • Manganese • Chromium • Tungsten •
        Molybdenum • Silicon • Nickel • Vanadium •
        Phosphorus and Sulfur
    Popular Knifemaking Steels 254
        W2 • O1 • L6 • A2 • F2 • M2 • D2 • 44OC •
        154CM • On Working With the Different Alloys

Index 267

Foreword

Knifemaking may strike you as a curious endeavor. With so many good knives available, you might ask, why would anyone want to make one by hand?

That very question coursed through my mind when a friend who worked in the office next to mine began talking to me about the knives he was making. Almost every day he would work the word knife into our conversations in some way. And samples of the different blades he was making would be placed casually on his desk, used as paperweights and letter openers.

I was surprised by the beauty and especially the uniqueness of those handmade knives. They were sleek and graceful, with a more personal and mellow look than commercial knives. I knew that my friend was strictly a beginner at this craft. And he had no great amount of experience in metal or woodworking, either. Yet after just a few weeks of experience, he was making beautiful knives.

Finally, his goading got to me, and I ordered a blade from a company selling knifemaking supplies. My initial project was not to make a whole knife, but just to fashion a handle for a blade that had been turned out by machine. Soon I was gluing, cutting, filing, grinding, and sanding away at my own knife project.

My knifemaking lasted perhaps a year, and I turned out three knives before directing my attention to other crafts and recreations. But I was happy to have had the experience, not so much because I made exceptional knives but because I was able to feel the relationship that develops between a person and a knife that is made for personal use.

A knife is perhaps the most basic and useful of all tools. Most of us develop favorites among the knives we keep in our homes for kitchen use, gardening, sport, and carving. When you reach for a knife, you automatically feel for the one that you like, that has served you best in the past, or that has some unique attraction to you that is hard to explain.

When you have made a knife yourself and have shaped the blade just the way you want it and the handle is made to fit your own hand, a special relationship develops between you and that tool. David Boye says that effectively and even eloquently in this book, but putting the feeling into words captures only part of the experience. Just as you feel the handle of a knife, you also feel the specialness of a handle that is of your own making. And when you have ground and filed a blade to suit a purpose that is clear in your own mind, you have a special, more personal feeling when you use that blade.

In this age when we are flooded with machine-made products for almost every conceivable purpose, the experience of making and using your own special knife becomes more important. Making a knife is like fashioning a key to a wider awareness of your own abilities and relationship to tools. These days, we have too few such opportunities.

Robert Rodale

Preface

This is a book written by a beginner to help other beginners start out. The methods discussed in this book are simple ones which every knifemaker should know about. After mastering these techniques, you can develop many other knifemaking skills. The whole field of modern metallurgy offers opportunities to develop finer and finer blades. Knives can also be considered useful jewelry, and you can pursue advancement in this area according to your aesthetic sensitivities.

I am constantly changing and improving my own craft. It seems that every new batch of knives is noticeably improved over its predecessor. I have no idea what my knives will be like in a year or two or three. Thus, for me, at least, knifemaking is growth itself.

Francine Martin helps me in every way and has been a major factor in my knifecraft, as well as with the book itself. She also has done most of the etchings of my knives, helped guide our other artists, and helped to develop our business.

Dennis Bodewitz, my fellow knifemaker, is great to work with and constantly upgrades the quality of our knives. Knifemaking is growth for him also.

Rosemarie Manlove has typed and proofread the manuscript, making a beautiful copy from a tangled mass of scribbles. What would we have done?

Rosemary Balsley has typed the later additions to the manuscript.

Bruce Tanner helped develop our sheathmaking technique.

Leslie Knowlton developed and printed my photos. These are mostly sheathmaking photos and pictures of knives. Franklin Avery also took some of the pictures of knives. Grant Heidrich photographed most of the knifemaking-process shots.

The etchings on the knives shown in this book were done by Francine Martin, Jessie Oster, Joyce Sierra, and Andra Rudolf.

Introduction

Nearly every adult uses a knife almost every day. If not at work, then in the gathering and preparation of food. But how many knives does one see that are genuine works of loving craftsmanship? Very few, if any. Individually made knives are so rare in this country that I have seen only a few examples other than those that I or one of my associates have made. Now, it strikes me that the potential market for beautiful handmade knives should be near to the demand for, say, handmade pottery; and yet there are thousands of potters and only a handful of knifemakers. Why? I believe this is due to two factors: first, making and marketing knives is complex and exacting, and not everyone can conjure up the variety of skills required or sustain this kind of energy output; second, and far more important, there is scant information available to the public on knifemaking techniques, and even less about small-time production of quality knives. It is one thing to make one knife, or ten knives, and quite another to make knives every working day as a means of livelihood. A whole new set of skills is required for the production of a large enough number of individually crafted knives to be able to earn a living.

Prior to this century, the art of making good knives and swords was a matter of great social importance. The production of high-quality blades was an essential aspect of weaponry and a good sword on the battlefield was strictly a matter of life and death. The effectiveness of governments and armies was dependent upon this art. Because of the great importance which has been attached to the knowledge of forging and tempering blades, and in the smeltering of the steels, the craft has been surrounded by an aura of mystery. As a means of gaining personal power, individual blacksmiths would cloak their work in secrecy and imply that their products were superior to their competitors in some occult way. Thus, it was a cheap and successful trick which kept the techniques of smeltering and tempering in the minds and hands of relatively few. Surprisingly, today we still find both aspects of this syndrome; a public with the general belief (however foggy and uncertain this belief is) that the methods of making good blades are esoteric, and somehow beyond them, and the members of the profession subtly reinforcing this general attitude. Perhaps here we can account for some of the disparity between the supply and demand for handmade knives.

Whether or not this is always true, one thing is certain—it takes a lot of hard work to learn to make one good knife, and once you know how, it is still a lot of work to make one good knife.

So now we come to the question of the hour—why bother? The most direct answer is that it is possible to make knives that are technically superior to those you can buy in the store, provided you have a very good piece of steel to start with (or the proper metals to smelter) and that you have the proper techniques and skills. But technical superiority is not the major reason why people hand-make knives, nor is it why people are willing to pay rather surprising amounts of money for them. Handmade knives are unique, reflecting the skills and personality of their maker. They impart a personal touch to what would be a cold, impersonal item. Thus it is with a handmade knife, or a handmade article of any kind, that there is a subtle exchange of electromagnetic energy that is transferred from the heart and the hands of the craftsman to the heart of the person who sees and uses the handmade article. Hopefully, the product will be the embodiment and expression of love and beauty in a useful, sanitary, and safe cutting tool—a hint of a deeper, more profound spirit in the process of living. The knife is held in the hand and is the most primary of tools. We use the knife to gather and prepare much of our food. We find in this most intimate linkup between the hand and the mouth an opportunity to enhance the subjective quality of life itself.

A knife is first a tool. But if it is also beautiful and contains within its vibratory structure the love of its maker, then this love is put into the food we eat and into the work we do. This constant subtle reminder of love in association with the daily food and work can infuse a spiritual warmth into life that otherwise might have been of an impersonal, mechanical nature.

With this book I am presenting some simple techniques and instructions for making knives. I also include helpful information on the small-scale production of handmade knives. You can use this book to make one or several knives, or you can use it as a handbook to set up a cottage workshop and eventually earn a living with the craft.

If you are, indeed, using this book as a guide for knifemaking, let me suggest that you first read the entire book, cover to cover, as though it were a novel. Once familiar with the entire range of considerations, you can begin in a step-by-step fashion to realize your knifemaking goals.

A three-fingered 2-inch
utility knife with a lignum
vitae handle.

Chapter 1

Starting Out

To ease you into knifemaking let me tell you a little about my own experiences in starting out as a knifemaker. I will tell you how I made my first knife, which I still use, and how you can make one like it. This puts the process in the simplest possible terms and will serve as a springboard for you to move into the more arcane aspects of knifemaking, just as it did for me.

The First Knife

A number of years ago after dropping out of graduate school in search of what I hoped would be a simpler and more meaningful life, I was faced with the need to acquire money, on a regular basis. I wanted my work to be useful, and beautiful, and most important, my own. I had spent the first thirty years of my life pleasing other people, and now I wanted to please myself. But, what could I do?

Even though I had no training and very little practice at working with my hands, I decided that I would like to make hand tools, such as chisels, hammers, pliers, and perhaps some knives. So I scrounged up a few tools out of the junk pile. I already had a cutting and welding torch, and a friend of mine had practically given me a fine bench grinder, so, with this basic set-up, I was in the tool-making business. What shall I make first? What *can* I make? I happened to have an old two-man saw, leaning up against the corner of my house, rusting away, certain never to be put to work again. Having heard that saw blades could be made into good knives, the thought occurred that I could make a good knife out of that useless steel. I had an old Chinese chopping knife that I used in the kitchen, and I considered it a valuable tool, so I decided to make a knife of that style. My Chinese knife had a solid wooden handle that was attached to a long shank which protruded from the body of the blade. It had a full width of steel running all the way through the handle, making it stronger and easier to make. I would later learn that this design is called a full-tang handle by knifemakers.

Tracing the silhouette onto the blade was easy. Using a nail, I scratched it into the rust on the old two-man. But cutting it out was impossible because of that damned rust! So, with some heavy sandpaper and kerosene, I cleaned the surface of the old saw and started over.

But now tracing the silhouette onto the clean steel was a problem. A nail wouldn't scratch it, white chalk wouldn't show up, and my daughter's crayon would melt away and totally disappear with the approach of the cutting torch tip. I finally blackened the surface of the steel with the acetylene torch flame and scratched the outline on with a pointed stick.

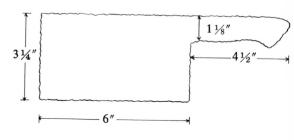

I cut out this shape and wound up with a "blank."

There would have to be some holes through the handle (or tang) for the rivets that would secure the handle. That posed no problem, though; I just blew some holes in the steel with the cutting torch.

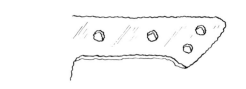

I went to work with a bench grinder cleaning the jagged edges left by the cutting torch. I ground them away so that the silhouette of the knife was completely clean, shaped just the way I wanted it.

I took another good look at the way it was ground. How thin it was and how far up the grind went. I noticed that the blank's edge, along where it was cut, no longer had a silver color, but had turned a beautiful blue with a nice rainbow effect. I knew this indicated that the steel had lost some of its "temper"

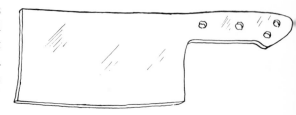

or hardness. Having only the vaguest idea of the tempering process, as well as thinking that the knife would work pretty well even without this treatment, I decided to wait and tackle this problem on some future knife. In retrospect, it was a wise decision.

I then began grinding the blade on the bench grinder. (If you don't know exactly what a bench grinder looks like, check in the section on tools.) First, I "hollowed out" steel along the cutting edge, so that a cross-section of the blade looked as shown.

Then I trimmed the steel right along the edge of the blade so that the sides of the grind were nice and even from the hollow part clear to the edge.

I tried very hard to keep the grinding even. I found that I was aided in this by resting the blade on the grinder's work rest and running the edge back and forth along it. As soon as I thought the edge was thin enough, I sharpened the blade on the grinder and immediately went into the kitchen and tried out the blade, to see if it was the right thickness.

To my surprise, the Chinese knife was much thinner than the one that I had ground, and seemed to cut much better, so I proceeded to grind the blade as thin as I dared. Fortunately, I didn't grind it so thin that it became brittle.

I then took a long look at the blade, which was very rough and coarse, covered with heavy grinding lines and rust pits left over from its previous life as a rusty saw blade. I knew I had to polish the blade somehow so I started with a medium grade of sandpaper. After about a half an hour, I realized I wasn't getting anywhere, so I put down the sandpaper and pondered this latest problem. Obviously I needed some kind of grinder that was smoother than the stone on the bench grinder and more powerful than hand-powered sandpaper. I went on a minor rampage, looking through everything on hand until I came across a small electric hand drill with a sanding attachment. I

went down to the local country store and bought a packet of sanding discs for it and resumed my task with new zeal.

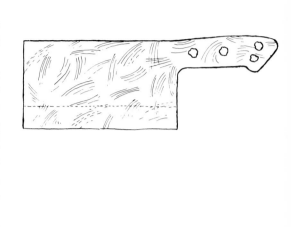

This time it worked. The rough disc I tried first slowly removed the blemishes, but left circular blemishes that were almost as unsightly. The answer to this problem was right in the packet of sanding discs: a finer-grit sanding disc. In a mere two hours, I was able to remove all the ugly pits and coarse grinding marks from the side of the blade by using finer and finer grits. I cleaned the handle area so it would be clean for the glue.

While I was performing these steps, I was quietly wondering how I was going to make the handle.

I decided to make the handle out of an old dry apple branch that had broken from a tree about two years previously. I knew that wood would be well seasoned, beautiful, and very durable. Lucky for me, it was summer, and the wood was *dry*.

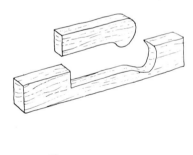

I knew I would glue the handle "slabs" on with cobbler's cement, because I had some, and epoxy glue had not yet come into my life. (The "slabs" are the two pieces of handle wood.) But I had no idea what I would use for rivets, so as soon as I finished polishing the blade I again ransacked my junk pile. I found an old car radio antenna. Since car antennas are actually chrome-plated brass tubing, I seized upon the plan of using the tubing as pins and flairing the ends of the tubing with a punch, ever so neatly, without splitting the wood, so that the widened ends of the pins would hold the handle slabs tightly in place.

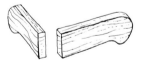

Before doing this, though, I double-checked to make sure that the piece of tubing actually fit the holes I had made in the tang. If it hadn't, I simply would have used the torch to enlarge the holes.

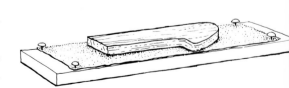

I was now ready to make the handle. Using a coping saw (see section on tools), I cut a piece of wood into a single block about ¾ inch thick. It was the exact silhouette of the handle on my chopping knife. I also left a little room for error.

Next, I cut the piece of handle wood right down the middle, forming two slabs. I made the inside of the slabs, where they join with the steel, perfectly flat. I did this by rubbing the slabs against a piece of sandpaper tacked to a board.

Here's where I made a big mistake. I should have rounded off the front part of the slabs and polished that area with fine sandpaper. This should be done before the handle goes on the blade. I ended up really marring the blade's finish with scratches trying to sand this area after the slabs had already become part of the knife.

At this point I thought I would be ready to glue the slabs onto the tang, but something was wrong: the holes that I had blown into the tang with the cutting torch didn't match up with the holes in the handle slabs.

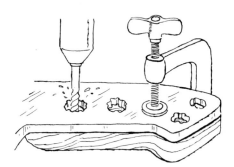

The obvious answer was to glue one side on first, drill through the holes cut in the steel, then glue the other slab on and drill it from the side now drilled correctly. I was a little embarrassed to drill the holes in this fashion at first, because it seemed so elementary and awkward. But do you know, to this day, I still drill each slab separately through the holes in the steel first.

I drilled the holes through the slabs in the above-mentioned manner, first gluing and drilling one side, and then the other. It turned out that as shiny as the tang looked, it was still coated with a thin layer of oil, preventing the cement from holding. I overcame this little setback by using gasoline and a fresh cloth to clean off the tang and the inside of the slab prior to gluing.

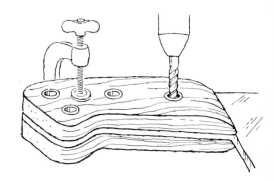

I used cobbler's cement to glue the slabs to the tang, waiting until it dried to tap in the tubing pins. After applying the glue, I clamped the slabs tightly against the tang with two or three C clamps.

After the glue dried, I removed the clamps and roughly shaped the handle using a rasp. I used a very coarse, rounded-off grinding wheel on the bench grinder to shape my first handle and progressively finer grits of sandpaper to fine-finish.

When I had the handle about two-thirds finished, I carefully flaired the ends of the tubing pins with a punch. At this point I did something that I thought was quite clever. I hammered little sections of very heavy copper wire into the holes of the tubing pins, and then I ground them flush. I did this to all except the one rivet nearest the butt end of the handle, which I left open to lace a piece of leather through.

Next I buffed the entire knife, handle and all, on a buffing wheel which I put on the bench grinder. I used "stainless" buffing compound, which is fast-cutting for steel and leaves a high "color" or lustre on both steel and wood. And, finally, I very carefully ground an edge on the blade, first using the grindstone, then an ordinary kitchen whetstone.

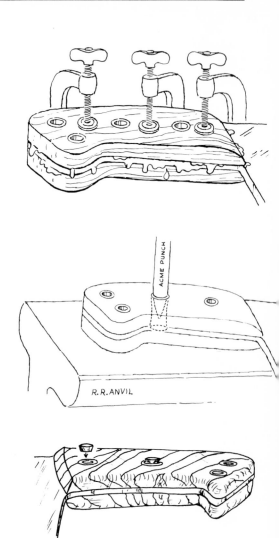

What Is a Good Knife?

Before we go any further, we need to step back and look at the whole phenomenon of knives and people. As with anything, there must be as many different attitudes and value structures regarding knives as there are people. Therefore, this book can only be of maximum value if you utilize this insight and information according to your needs, desires, and values.

Knives, of course, can be anything from a shoddy dime-store item to a powerful tool or weapon, or an exquisite work of functional (or nonfunctional) art. How good any knife is, depends solely upon the values of the user.

The merit of a knife is really based upon how well it lives up to your expectations. You might really like a

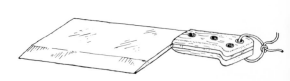

knife that you paid two dollars for ten years ago and that has held up well for its cost, and you may, on the other hand, dislike a "better-quality" knife that is really too heavy to carry or that doesn't hold an edge as well as it should. Or you might prefer a simple knife with an old wooden handle over a modern, high-performance, corrosion-resistant model that to you appears to be the product of a chrome and computer age. And, obviously, another knife fancier could see it just the other way around.

The point is that you, the user, or you, the knifemaker, are the ultimate judge.

Design

This factor is discussed at length in chapter 3. Suffice it to say that a knife should look beautiful (to you) and should feel comfortable in your hand when you use it. It should be strong enough but not overly heavy. Excess weight is one of the most subtle but most telling faults of many knives, especially those which are designed to be carried, either in the pocket or a sheath.

The design of the knife should be such that the "movement," or flow, of lines, mass, and weight, as well as the physical strength of the materials and the keenness of the edge should all work together as a "transmitter" of energy, from the hand of the user to the cutting edge. The design is the physical expression of the intended purpose of the knife.

Workmanship

Workmanship is how well the materials have been prepared and joined together to form the knife. It also implies the range of techniques that the maker has at his or her disposal. Here are some basic points of good workmanship. I will repeat them as each step arises in the text of the book. First, the grinding on the blade, as well as on all contours, should be smooth, sharp, and well defined. No obvious marks should remain from any of the processes unless they have some decorative function. There should be no ripples in the blade.

All joints should be flush and smooth. There should be virtually no openings between materials, since any gap, such as between the slabs and the tang, can collect food and moisture. In addition to being unsightly and unsanitary, gaps are a seat of rust and rot, which, in the long run, will destroy the knife.

The knife should be straight along the blade line, from the butt to the tip.

The blade should be the right thickness, and heat-treated properly. These are somewhat more difficult points of judgment, but with some practice you can learn to really evaluate the merits of a blade.

Materials

To discuss materials is to speak technically. It doesn't do much good to tell you that a knife should be made of good steel, with handle materials that are beautiful, warm, strong, durable, and moisture-resistant. You already know that.

This entire book is about how to produce quality in knives, from all three standpoints; design, workmanship, and materials. Reading the whole book will make you a better judge of knives, but you must remember that the more you contemplate knives, the better judge of knives you will become.

User's versus Collector's Knives

This is a distinction in quality and intended purpose among knives that people who are really into knives have found useful. A user's knife is one that is made with the intent of being used, and eventually worn out and thrown away.

Collector's knives, on the other hand, are so finely made, and so expensive, that they would generally not be used for practical work. They are usually prominently (or subtly) displayed.

The boundary between these two types of knives is quite fuzzy, and what would be a user's knife for one person might well be a prime collector's item for another.

A Knifemaker's Overview

I am going to briefly outline the knifemaking process described in this book so you will have a

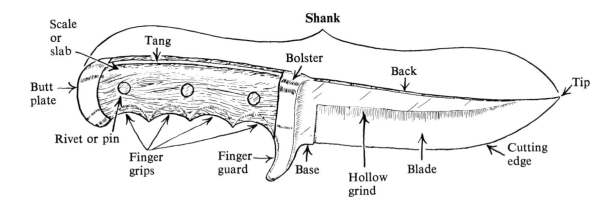

perspective of what we are going to cover, and so that we have something to relate to when I describe the tools recommended for the job. First, the steel is selected and cleaned. The knife is designed and the rough shape is drawn and cut out either with a cutting torch or with a band saw fitted with a special hard-metal cutting blade. The edges are trimmed and the shape further refined on the grindstone. Then the edge is roughly ground with the grindstone and refined on a belt grinder. The bolster and/or butt plate, if any, is braised on. Next, the knife is hardened, and then annealed in two ways. After that, the knife is further ground and polished with the belt grinder. The rivet holes are drilled, and etching, if any, is done at this point. The wooden, bone, or micarta handles are drilled, glued, and riveted. The handle is shaped on the belt grinder and put through a series of progressively finer abrasive treatments; the entire knife is buffed on a flannel wheel; and the blade is sharpened on a fine belt and the buffing wheel. Finally, the handle is treated with oil and the knife is inspected and signed. (A complete list of the steps involved is given on page 199.)

Basic Skills

One of the main difficulties for the person who wants to make one or two knives, as well as those just beginning the trade, is gaining access to the proper tools and keeping them in good working order. This takes some mechanical aptitude, especially in cases where machines are older or cheaply made. These machines may need modification even for small-time production work, and if you are not at first handy in diagnosing the noise and vibration of an electric machine, you will be after making several knives. Many junior colleges and trade schools offer classes in small machine or general shop that include fundamentals of electric wiring, welding, grinding, buffing, et cetera. This would be helpful in setting up your shop, in knowing which tools you need to use for what operations, and in learning to recognize good quality tools.

"Handmade" does not mean "inefficient," and, if you need to make a living, even a modest one, you have got to keep things moving. Face facts; unless you are an expert, read basic texts on the following subjects, plus anything else you think is relevant:

Oxyacetylene cutting and welding
Simple tool machining and metallurgy
Electrical wiring
Electrical motors

You will discover many ways to increase your effectiveness and the efficiency and life of your tools by reading a few simple books on these subjects. I will try to tell you everything else you need to know about making knives by the method of grinding and heat-treating (not forging).

What Is a Good Blade?

At first glance, this seems to be a pretty simple question, deserving a simple, direct answer. But actually I am finding that the more I delve into the different criteria and metallurgical possibilities for blades, the more complicated the question becomes. For this reason I will give you two answers: first, a simple, straightforward one that will satisfy most people enough so that they can go ahead and make some knives. Then, in the appendix, I will provide a more complete answer, involving some of the different types of alloy steels and some of the more subtle possibilities of steel chemistry and design. The appendix will give you an idea of how iron, carbon, and the various alloys, as well as some different heat-treatment processes, produce the different qualities in steel.

Here is the simple, straightforward answer: A good blade must first be shaped properly and ground to the proper thickness so that it cuts well in the operations for which it is designed. These factors are discussed in chapter 3. It should also be noted that the factors of blade design and thickness interact to some extent with the type of steel and the tempering processes used.

The second factor in a good blade is the character of the steel used. There are four factors having to do with steel service. Simply stated, they are: hardness, toughness, wear resistance, and resistance to corrosion. *Hardness* is the tendency to resist indentation. *Toughness* is the elastic strength to resist deformation and fracture. *Wear resistance* is the ability to stand up under abrasive pressure. *Corrosion resistance*, as you might have guessed, is the ability to stand up under chemical attack, such as rust.

An ideal knife blade should be hard so that it won't become dented and scratched, tough enough so that it won't bend or break, and wear-resistant enough so that it will hold a good edge. (If it is too hard and too wear-resistant, it will be difficult to sharpen.) An ideal blade should also be "stainless" so that it won't darken and rust.

These four factors are interrelated and no ideal steel has yet been designed that produces the perfect blade. What you have is a series of trade-offs. For example, the harder a given steel is tempered, the more brittle it becomes. The same is generally true of wear resistance: the more wear resistance, the less toughness. Two steels of the same hardness may be very different in terms of wear resistance due to differing alloy makeup (steel design). Two pieces of the same alloy that have been hardened to the same degree can differ in toughness, due to differing heat-treatments. The subject is further complicated when you start getting into corrosion resistance and the so-called "stainless" steels. So you see, this whole thing is a Pandora's box. If you are interested, skip ahead to the appendix, Introduction to Alloy Steels.

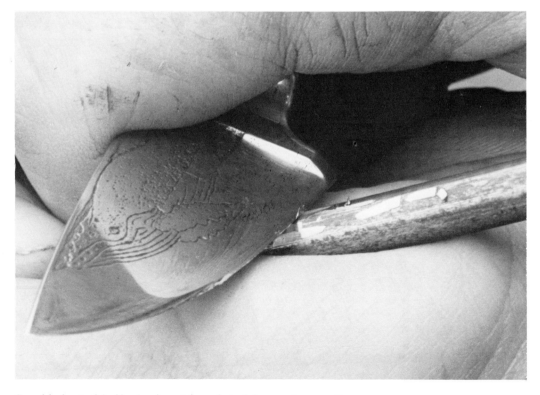

Saw-blade steel knife shaving strips of steel from a large nail, showing the difference in hardness between the two steels.

What Kind of Steel?

As a knifemaker, one of the decisions you have to make is the kind of steel you will choose for a particular knife. There are two vaguely defined categories to choose from. The first is ordinary carbon steel. This category includes steels that differ in the types and proportions of carbon and alloys that are mixed together with the iron. The things they have in common are that they all temper, i.e., become hardened, via the same basic series of treatments, and they will rust and corrode.

The second broad category could be described as the "exotic" or "alloy" steels. These materials have a wide variety of characteristics. One thing they all have in common is that each was designed to do something that plain carbon steel will not do. Some are designed to retain hardness at higher temperatures. Some, such as cobalt and carbide, can be made harder than ordinary carbon steel. Some are designed to resist corrosion and rust. Some of these have been adapted or designed for making knife blades. All these steels differ in terms of the treatments that make them hard and tough.

Because this book is about basic knifemaking, I have decided to limit the basic instructions to the use of carbon steel (AISI Numbers 01, W2, and saw-blade steel which is also known as L6 steel). With this traditional type of steel you can produce handsome, durable knives of very high quality, and at the lowest possible cost for materials. Exotic steels are briefly covered in the appendix.

Most knifemakers began their careers using carbon steel from old saw blades, files, or leaf-springs from cars.

Saw-blade Steel

Since used saw blades are fairly consistent metallurgically, come in a variety of ideal sizes and thick-

The author holding a section of band-saw blade.

nesses, and are very easy to obtain, I suggest that you use this wonderful source of steel, especially if you are a beginner. I have found that for the beginning knifemaker, and even for the advanced one, saw-blade steel is quite adequate. Once you have mastered making knives out of old saw blades you may then wish to experiment with other steels.

I use carbon saw-blade stock which I scrounge from lumber mills and scrap yards. These blades are made from top-quality carbon steel and are ideal for knifemaking. The following are some of the different types.

Band saw blades come in several thicknesses, up to twelve-gauge, which is a little over $3/32$-inch thick. These blades run 9 to 12 inches wide and approximately 45 feet long, so, if you get one, you can cut out a lot of knives. Twelve-gauge is a good weight for most of the heavier kitchen knives and for most lighter camping- and hunting-type knives, too. The thinner gauges, which are also easier to find, are good for fine paring, slicing, and fileting-type knives.

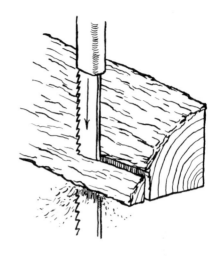

Drag saws, which have not been used commercially since the advent of chain saws, employ a blade thicker than the heaviest band blade (approximately 1/8 inch). These blades look something like the two-man hand saw, but are heavier and are shaped differently, like so.

These can still be found around junk piles and in steel yards. Because of their precise thickness, they are an excellent source of knife steel. They have a good weight for skinning and camping knives. They are also suitable for heavy kitchen knives, ranging from vegetable and carving knives to light cleavers.

There are lots of old *two-man saws* around that look like this.

They can be anywhere from 5 to 16 feet long. The thickness is right for fine vegetable knives, filet knives, and light sheath knives. There is great variability among these blades metallurgically.

The *circle saw* blades run up to about ¼ inch in thickness. These can provide the heavier hunting and skinning knives, meat cleavers, hatchets, and other tools, such as chisels.

Analysis of Saw-blade Steel

The steel used by a large manufacturer of lumber mill blades shows the following content: carbon .74 percent; silicon .25 percent; manganese .42 percent; potassium .025 percent; sulfur .011 percent; chrome .03 percent; and nickel 2.60 percent. The remaining portion of the steel is iron, plus some trace impurities. (See the appendix.)

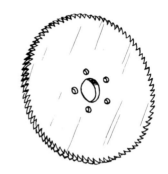

Most saw-blade steel probably falls into the L6-type category, which isn't surprising, because L6 is listed in *Tool Steels** as a favorite steel for making saw blades and knife blades. For more on L6 and other types of steel, see the appendix.

I have found that all carbon steel saw blades produce nearly the same edge-holding properties with uniform heat-treating, so I heat-treat all blades with the same process described in the tempering section, p. 116.

One type of saw blade that is commonly used for knifemaking, however, is in a special category. This is the *mechanical hacksaw blade*. Altogether, these blades look pretty much alike, but they are made from a wide variety of metals, and are generally not plain carbon steel. Therefore, they cannot be heat-treated with the techniques used for carbon steel. Using this steel is a little risky, since it is difficult to determine just what a particular mechanical hacksaw blade is made of. I have not attempted to cover the tempering instructions for these types of steel.

---

*   This volume, *Tool Steels*, by G. A. Roberts, J. C. Hamaker, Jr., and A. R. Johnson, first published in 1962, is the authoritive work on the subject. I recommend you order one, direct from the American Society for Metals, Metals Park, OH 44073.

Corrosion

One disadvantage of carbon steel saw-blade stock is that it is not stain-resistant, and therefore it can rust, especially if exposed to saltwater or salt air. It will certainly darken with age. Therefore, it is an individual question as to which steel to choose for making a knife. Who will use it? For what purpose and where will it be used? Is cost a factor?

Some people prefer carbon steel aesthetically, for its antique look, since it darkens over the years, and/or because they do not trust stainless steel. When stainless steel first came out, it was not suited for holding a good edge, but because of its noncorrosive properties many knives were produced from it, giving stainless a bad name. And, since many knives are made from even cheaper grades of stainless steel today, its reputation has become synonymous with poor quality to the general public.

Since this is really a book for beginners, I will present one general approach toward making knives from sheets of carbon steel. If you prefer to use some other materials, perhaps some highly wear-resistant tool steel, or one of the better high-carbon stainless steels on the market, you can still use this book. However, instead of referring to the tempering instructions and recommendations which are given in chapter 7, refer to the appendix. The general characteristics and heat-treating techniques for most commonly used "exotic" steels are presented there.

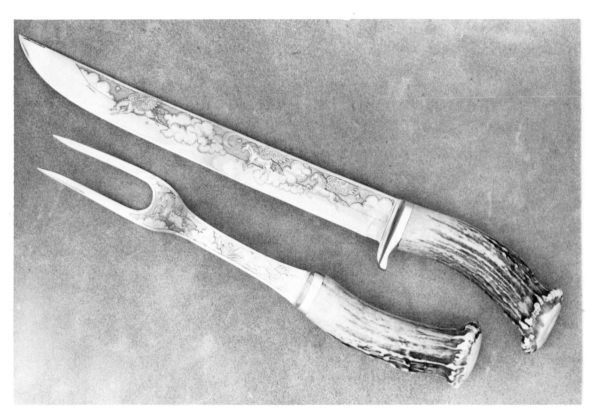

Horn-handled carving set with *Pegasus* etching by Jessie Oster.

Chapter 2

Tools

Obviously, the shop arrangements you need will be determined in part by the number and the quality of knives you plan to make. If you wish to make just a few knives, you can probably borrow or rent the machines you do not have. You may gain access to nearly any of the necessary tools by enrolling in a shop class in a high school or college. Or you can take your knives to someone's shop to do one or two operations on a machine that you don't have. If you have a small number of knives to make, you can do some of the operations by hand, or substitute a lighter duty machine. For example, you can cut out the handles with a coping saw instead of a band saw or a jigsaw. You can use a sanding block or rasp instead of a belt sander to shape the handle. Or you can purchase an inexpensive 3-inch drum sander that fits into the chuck of a power drill or on an arbor like a grinding wheel. It will do most of the operations of the belt grinder. You can harden knives with a cutting torch or in a small ceramic kiln or a forge. You need some kind of a grinder to get a hollow grind. You can polish the blade and shape the handle with a disc sander, either on a drill or a bench grinder, but this is very cumbersome and not likely to produce a satisfactory knife.

If you use the clumsier tools, such as a disc instead of a belt sander, you will, to some degree, diminish your own satisfaction with your work.

One thing I have learned the hard way is not to put much faith in tools that are cheaply made, or, for that matter, in tools that were acquired under questionable circumstances. Such tools can fail you at critical moments, but more likely—and more devastating—is that they will do a poor job. Besides dulling the shine of your craftsmanship, cheap tools will wobble and whine, and make the round edges square and the square ones round. And they'll bloody your fingers.

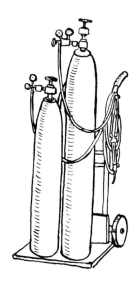

I am going to describe some of the tools that I use and tell you what I know about them in terms of what they do and how well they perform for *production knifemaking*, and you can determine how essential each one is to the type of knifemaking operation you have in mind. By production knifemaking, I mean being able to produce fifty or so knives per month, single-handed. I work in batches of knives of about ten to twenty per batch. This way I repeat each operation on each knife in the batch, then move to the next operation. I can still give each knife individual attention, but I don't have to start and stop the machines so often.

Oxyacetylene Torch

This is one of the most useful tools in any workshop. Not only can you use it for cutting out knives, tempering them and annealing them, but this tool is invaluable for fabricating and modifying other tools, such as making a good stand for your new belt grinder, for making a workbench, or heating some gear or bushing that won't come off its shaft, et cetera. The most useful type of setup is the "convertible" torch, like the one in the drawing. The cutting and welding tips are interchangeable on the same torch handle. Otherwise, when you change from the cutting tip to a welding tip, you have to unscrew the entire torch from the gas lines. If you have a cutting and a welding attachment, you can use steel freely as a medium from which to transform your dreams into reality.

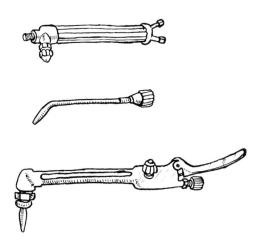

Motors and Power Application

There are several factors to consider when appointing a motor to perform a given task: the size, or horsepower (HP) rating, the direction of rotation, the operating revolutions per minute (RPM), and the electrical requirements.

I have mentioned the general horsepower requirements for the various machines in the sections below, but these requirements will depend greatly on the particular machine you are using and how hard you are going to push it. Most machines are driven by a V-belt drive mechanism consisting of the belt (or belts) and the pulleys on the motor and the machine. Depending on the relative size of the pulleys, the motor will produce more or less speed and inversely proportional torque (turning force) in the machine.

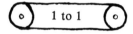

This works on the same principle as the different gears in an automobile transmission.

Each motor has a small metal plate on which the operating speed and horsepower rating is stamped. Most motors manufactured for workshop use run at either 1,750 RPM or 3,600 RPM. Therefore, the relative size of the pulleys chosen to transmit power from the motor to the machine will depend on the operating speed of the motor and the desired running speed of the machine.

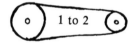

"Horsepower" is the ability to do a certain measured amount of work in a given amount of time (1 horsepower is 33,000 foot-pounds of work per minute). Therefore, if you connect a machine so that it is running twice as *fast* as the motor (2 to 1 ratio), then it can pull only half as *hard* against the workpiece.

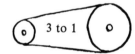

The factors to consider when making a motor connection are the desired "safe" speed of the machine and the power of the motor. You don't want the machine to exceed its safety limits and you don't want the motor to pull harder than it was designed to pull. If a motor is under too much working strain, it will burn out. If it is under too much starting strain, it may only burn out the motor-starting unit.

You can determine the operating speed of the machine by determining the motor speed and multiplying that by the ratio of the pulleys. For example, if it is a 1,750 RPM motor with a machine pulley one-half as large (in circumference) as the motor pulley (a 2 to 1 ratio), then the machine speed is $1,750 \times 2 = 3,500$ RPM. This can be further translated into feet per minute (FPM) by multiplying the circumference of the machine drive wheel (not the pulley) in inches times the RPM, divided by twelve.

Another factor when considering the best speed for a machine is vibrational chatter. This is especially true of older or more cheaply made machines. Due to a certain amount of looseness in the bearings and imbalance in the shaft or wheels, you may find a given machine is more "comfortable" to run at a speed somewhat below the "safety limit." Some machines are "in harmony" at a certain speed, but chatter at lower or higher speeds.

Variable Speed Machines

Variable speed functioning can be obtained from a single-speed motor by certain ways of setting up the power "transmission." This is especially desirable on such machines as the band saw and the drill press. The simplest method of accomplishing this is to use a multisize pulley (similar to the gear arrangement on a ten-speed bicycle), on either one or both ends of the V-belt. To be able to change the belt freely from one pulley size to the other, you need some way of loosening the belt and then taking up the slack. Here are two ways this may be accomplished. One method is to mount the motor on a hinge so it can be raised and lowered to accommodate the different pulley settings. For this setup, you need a belt sufficiently long that it can be slightly out of line without binding or causing too much friction.

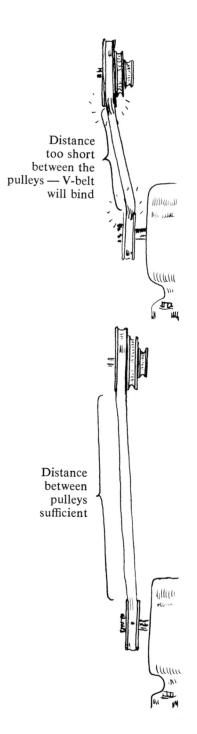

Distance too short between the pulleys — V-belt will bind

Distance between pulleys sufficient

Another way is to use a third member, or idler wheel, to take up the belt slack at the different settings. This third wheel can keep the belt tight by means of a spring or notch-adjusting mechanism.

There are more elaborate methods to produce a variable speed machine. For example, I have seen a washing machine motor transmission unit used on a 14-inch, 2-speed band saw.

Electric Power

There are three factors to consider in electricity: phase, voltage, and amperage. The limitations of your shop wiring and the power requirements of your lights and motors must follow strictly the dictates of these factors. If the machines are not correctly wired, you will blow a fuse or circuit breaker. But you may as easily ruin a good motor, cause a fire, or risk dangerous electric shock. This is one area where it is important to play by the rules. The electrical requirements of each motor are stamped on the identification plate.

Phase

Generally, electricity will be either single-phase or three-phase. Single-phase is used for residential power and some light industry. Three-phase is used to power production industry because it is more efficient. We don't need to go into the technical differences between the two types of power. Suffice it to say that if you can get three-phase, use it. Be sure that you run three-phase motors only on three-phase juice and single-phase motors on single-phase juice.

Voltage

This is a measure of "electrical pressure" available, like water pressure. Most residential and light industrial electricity is 110 volts or 110–220 volt. Do not try to run a 110-volt motor with 220 volts, or vice

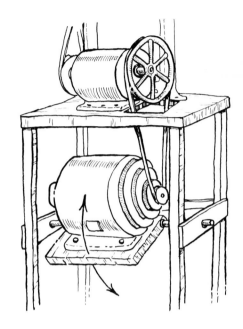

versa. If your motor is 110–220 volt, make sure it is properly wired for the type of electricity available to your shop. The same 110–220 volt motor will require twice as much amperage if it is used at 110 volts rather than at 220 volts.

Amperage (amp)

This is a measure of the flow of electricity. It is analogous to the amount of water flowing through a faucet. While the voltage in a system is essentially constant, the amperage varies according to the "pull" of the electrical fixture.

Each circuit is "fused" according to the amount of amperage it can safely carry. This may be done either with fuses or with circuit breakers. In either case, they are labeled in accordance with their maximum amperage. If you draw more than this through the circuit, the fuse will blow or the breaker will break.

Now, what you need to do is check the amperage of each of your electrical circuits, making sure your total draw is less. Go around and add up the total number of amps on all the motors and lights that will be running simultaneously from a given circuit. For lights, figure about one amp for every 100 watts. You may need to bring in an extra line if you have a number of people working together in the same shop.

Motors draw the most electricity when they are starting or when they are under a heavy load. They may draw more than their amp rating in these conditions. If two people turn on two motors at the same time, the fuse may blow.

Wiring

"Wire gauge" is the diameter of the electrical conductor. The smaller the number, the larger the wire and the greater its current-carrying capacity. The insulation has nothing to do with the current-carrying capacity, but merely keeps the wires apart so they do not "short."

Current-carrying capacities for a variety of gauges in common use:

These values assume a maximum cable length of 50 feet. Go to the next larger gauge for each 100 feet.

18 gauge	=	4.5 amps
16 gauge	=	9.0 amps
14 gauge	=	17.0 amps
12 gauge	=	20.0 amps
10 gauge	=	30.0 amps

Use three-wire cable, plugs, and receptacle. The third wire (green), and the large prong on the connector, are the safety ground. If a hot wire (one of the other two) somehow comes in direct contact with the motor housing and you touch the motor or any metal that is touching the "grounding" motor, you will receive a message from the angels. Be sure the motor is properly connected to the green ground wire and that the receptacle is properly wired to a good ground, such as a water pipe.

High-speed Grinders

You need a pretty good grinder to do production knife work. A grindstone either on an extra-long shaft of an electric motor or on the shaft of an arbor that is turned by a motor will do. The stone turns toward the operator so that the sparks fly downward. A wheel about 1 inch or 1½ inches seems to be optimum, but anything from 1 inch to 2 inches will serve. I use wheels that are anywhere from 8 to 14 inches in diameter. If the shaft diameter of your grinder is 1 inch or more, you can find many of the industrial castoff wheels at flea markets or local junk stores. The motor for a good grinder should be at least ½ horsepower, but preferably ¾ or 1 horsepower.

Grinding Wheel Safety

Grinding wheels have been known to fly apart causing fatal injury. This is because they are made of a baked ceramic-like substance which can crack like pottery. Therefore, you should take certain precautions to avoid injury. Obviously, don't use a wheel you think may have been dropped or hit. You can have old wheels tested for a fee, but I usually just look the wheel over well for severe chips which may indicate damage. I tap the wheel lightly to see if it sounds solid. It should have a subtle, but definite ring to it. Then I put it on the machine and stand back. If possible, I increase the speed to about one-half again faster than the operating speed. If it passes all of these tests, I start working with it, though cautiously at first. I don't necessarily recommend this test procedure; it is just what I do. Remember, an exploding wheel can easily kill you.

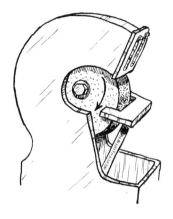

Your machine should also have a heavy metal safety shroud with a stop. A shroud or guard without a stop provides no protection against broken pieces which can fly around inside the guard and come flying out at you. Wear a heavy leather apron, goggles, and/or a face shield, too.

A respirator keeps you from inhaling too much dust, which can cause silicosis and shredding of lung tissue with loss of breath. Many old-time knifemakers and blacksmiths sound like they have lung troubles from the dust and smoke of their work.

Grinding Arbor

The best grinders are ball-bearing or roller-bearing arbors with a strong electric motor connected by a V-belt. An arbor is a shaft supported by two bearings and threaded at either end to hold the wheels. This type is better than a grinder with the wheel right on the motor shaft because it offers more freedom around the wheel and may have adjustable speeds.

A motor-only type grinder may be awkward because the knife blade, or your hands, may tend to bump the motor while working. However, with a motor-only type, if you have a wheel on each end of the motor, you can use one wheel for one side of the blade and the other for the opposite side, thus working around the motor bulk.

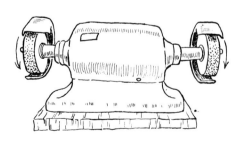

The arbor shaft should be heavy—a 1-inch or a 1¼-inch diameter is ideal, heavy enough to be very stable and to accommodate large stones.

Proper Direction for the Tightening Threads

In setting up or making an arbor, the tightening nut should be threaded so that as the grindstone tends to twist backward on the shaft while grinding, the movement twists the nut tighter, not looser. The connection between the wheel and the tightening nut tends to move the nut tighter if the threads are in the right direction, and vice versa.

Force exerted by the workpiece tends to move the wheel backwards in relation to the shaft

The Work Rest

There should be a small but strong adjustable work rest that fits the face of the wheel snugly. You should be able to adjust it in and out, up and down, and sideways. The angle and position of this work rest changes with the wheel size, so it is convenient to be able to adjust the angle of the work rest. The work rest should have little arms extending on either side beyond the face of the wheel, so you won't need the work rest very snug against the wheel. This prevents the blade from becoming caught between the work rest and wheel.

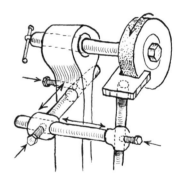

Pressure Guide for Production Grinding

For pressure-feeding the larger blades against the face of the wheel, I have made an adjustable pressure plate from an old and inexpensive vise. This produces a very even grind at a much faster rate than possible by hand.

You don't need this adjustable pressure plate at first, but you may later on. It has cut my grinding time by more than half for large knives, and, after working out all of the bugs, it produces a very even grind. Since the element forcing the blade against the wheel is a piece of steel, and not a hand or leather glove, the

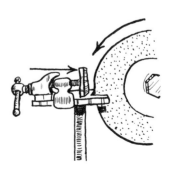

blade can be easily worked while hot, another time-saving advantage.

Grinding Wheels

Grinding wheels are graded according to the size of the abrasive particles imbedded in the body of the wheel. Small numbers (grit size) refer to large, coarse particles, and should be used for fast, rough grinding operations. Small-grit-size wheels produce slower, finer grinding work.

Grinding wheels are also graded according to the hardness of the wheel, and this determines how fast the wheel will cut and how long the wheel will last. Generally, a very soft wheel will cut very fast but will not last long, while a hard wheel will last longer but will not cut very fast. The softer wheel wears away faster, continually exposing new and sharp abrasive particles. You can get pretty good at determining these characteristics in wheels just by looking at them.

I use coarse-grit, hard wheels to do cleanup and rough grinding. I do the fine grinding with a belt machine.

Always keep the wheel well dressed and clean with a wheel dresser. I give my wheel a light treatment with the dresser after every five minutes or so of grinding.

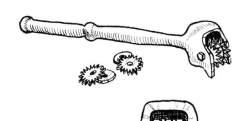

Wheel dresser

Belt Sander/Grinders

When working wood, this machine is called a sander; when working metal, it is called a grinder.

I spend much more time on the belt grinder than I do on the wheel grinder, perhaps more time than on all the other tools combined. It is used for grinding and polishing the blades as well as shaping and sanding the handles.

Controlling the Belt

The most important aspect of a belt grinder,

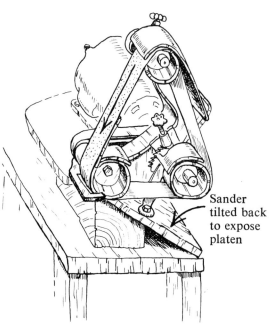

Sander tilted back to expose platen

Three-wheel belt sander

aside from power (at least ½ horsepower), is that it tracks the belts accurately. Sometimes you want the belt to track precisely on center, and sometimes you want the belt to lap over ⅛, ¼, or maybe ½ inch. The belt should overlap the wheel so you can work over the edge of the wheel and get into tight areas such as finger grips, et cetera.

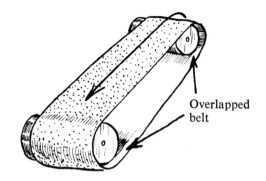

Overlapped belt

You also need clearance around the wheel just as you did with the wheel grinder. Most of the work on the belt sander will be done against the wheel, not on the flat surface.

There are two-, three-, and four-wheel belt grinders, from small table sanders to large industrial machines. Most any table-model belt sander will be useful in knifemaking, but for production work certain features are important. The first is a *positive tracking device* that will hold the belt exactly where you want it—a rounded-surface tracking wheel helps do this. Also, *ball bearings* are preferable over sleeve bearings because as the sleeve bearings become even a little loose, precise tracking becomes difficult.

Exposed bearing

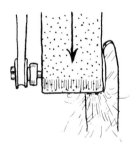

Clearance

The belt sander with the front wheel suspended on a stud is preferable to bearings on each side of the wheel because there is complete clearance to get at certain areas of the workpiece.

My first belt sander was a 6-inch by 48-inch machine. I now use both a 2-inch by 48-inch machine and a 2-inch by 72-inch machine. A 2-inch belt, which is useful for reaching hard-to-reach areas of the knife, is preferable over much wider belts.

Abrasive Belts

The abrasive quality of the belts, as with sandpaper, is caused by small shards of some material, such as rock, aluminum oxide, emery, or even diamond, that are glued to the surface of the cloth or paper. The abrasive material is graded by the grit-particle size and by the thickness of cloth or paper backing. Use only cloth belts for knifemaking. Paper belts are too weak and will tear before you get full use from them.

Considerably more expensive belts have a special coating that enable them to be run wet without falling apart. These belts also require a specially constructed water sander to apply the water and gather the runoff. This machine is better than a "dry" machine for working tempered blades because the water keeps the blades cool so they don't "lose their temper." (See Water-cooled Belt Grinder, p. 207.)

The Platen or Work Wheel

The wheel you work against is called the "platen." This drum underneath the belt should be covered with rubber so it will have some "give" to it. If yours does not, then you should cover the wheel with a coating of fairly hard rubber. One way to do this is to glue a layer of hard rubber onto the wheel with contact cement or epoxy glue. This must be done very carefully and evenly, and the rubber seam should be at an angle so it won't jump when you work against it.

Buy some hard rubber, say ¼-inch thick, from a tool supply house, and glue this to the platen. While

Belt too wide   Belt just right

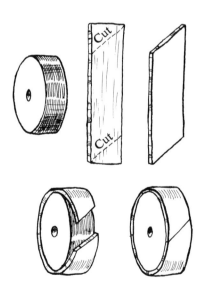

the epoxy is hardening, wrap the rubber tightly against the drum with many layers of twine, then remove the twine.

On my newer machine, I have two interchangeable rubber-coated wheels; one very hard, which is perfectly flat and with very square edges, and one made from softer rubber, with a very slightly rounded face and edges. I use these wheels for different belt-grinding and sanding operations. I use the hard, flat-faced wheel for the initial grinding, removing the stock from the hollow grind, and in those instances when I want to remove a lot of stock fast. I also use this wheel to cut sharp lines where the grinding stops at the base of the blade. The hard rubber wheel cuts cleaner, cooler, and more deeply.

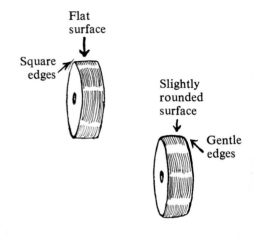

When I want smooth grinding during the final grinding and polishing steps, or when I am working the wood handles, or anytime I am overlapping the belt to work into corners, I use the softer, very slightly rounded wheel. You can shape a rubber wheel the way you want it with sandpaper (when the machine is running, belt off), or build it up with electrician's tape.

You may want the wheel slightly rounded off on one edge for smooth work, and very square on the other for sharply defined cutting.

Work Rest

A little U-shaped platform, just like the one described in the grinder section, is useful on the belt sander for grinding and polishing perfectly straight cuts on the longer blades. A work rest would be extremely useful on the 1- to 2-inch machines, but more awkward on a 4- to 6-inch machine.

Sleeve-type Drum Sanders

When I first started knifemaking, I did not have a belt sander. What I used to refine the grinding and to polish the blades was a 3-inch sleeve-type drum

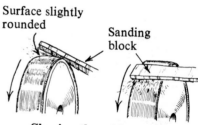

Shaping the rubber wheel

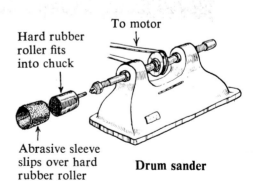

Drum sander

sander mounted on an inexpensive threaded arbor by means of a drill chuck.

This contrivance works well for making just a few knives, since the abrasive sleeves wear out quickly and you cannot guide the tracking of the sleeve as you could a belt. The sleeves are also quite expensive compared with other forms of abrasives.

Abrasive Strip Drum Sanders

A drum sander that uses a sleeve is much less economical than one that uses an abrasive strip. In the latter type, a strip of abrasive is wrapped around the outside of the drum and clamped in where the wheel splits.

This allows the knifemaker to buy the abrasive in 50-foot rolls at substantial savings, since it is far cheaper than the per-foot price of abrasive belts.

You can overlap the lip of the wheel with the belt on a belt sander for working in and around machine corners, but with a drum sander you cannot. You can also track the belt to different positions while the machine is running. However, a drum sander is very inexpensive and will certainly get you by for a while. You may even prefer the economy of the splitting-type drum sander over a belt grinder for regrinding the blades.

It is possible to have two or more drum sanders going at the same time, each with different size abrasive grit. This way, instead of stopping the machine to change grit size, you just move from wheel to wheel.

The "Flap-sander"

A reciprocating metal drum holds little flaps of abrasive strips that slap against the workpiece when the tool spins. Since there is no firm backing to the abrasive action, this treatment imparts a fluid quality to the surface. I use this machine mainly for the last treatment of the wood, micarta, or bone handles, prior to buffing.

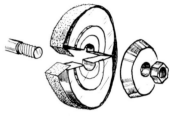

Abrasive strip sander
(*Open*)

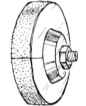

With belt in place

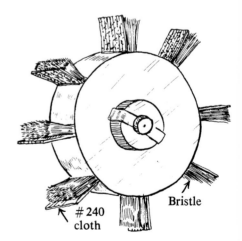

#240 cloth

Bristle

Flap-sander

There are several different types of flap sanders on the market. The most economical type uses separate replaceable rolls of abrasive strip, allowing you to wind out some more when the abrasive wears down. When the strips are used up, you simply refill.

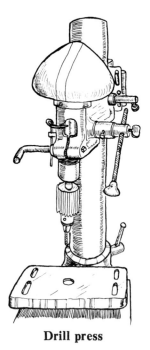

Drill press

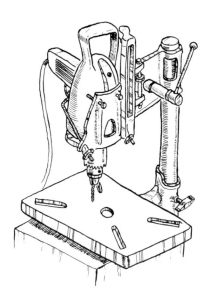

Other Equipment

Drill Press

An ordinary bench-type drill press is quite adequate for knifemaking. It is preferable for it to have at least two speeds: low speed for metal and high speed for wood.

If you do not have a drill press, but do have an electric hand drill, you can get a drill press frame that has a clamp to hold a hand drill. These are inexpensive and work well enough to get you by.

Band Saw

The band saw cuts out wood handles and splits them down the middle. It also mills knife handles out of larger pieces of wood and from pieces of stump (burl). However, for the first job a good table jigsaw will get you by.

If the band saw has a multispeed arrangement, you can use a very slow speed (500 feet per minute) for cutting out brass pieces, and possibly, if it runs as slow as 150 FPM, for cutting out the blades themselves. (To compute FPM, see section on electric motors, p. 22.)

A very large band saw is useful for milling large pieces of wood, but, for the most part, a 10-inch or a 12-inch two-wheel band saw will get you by.

Watch out for the four-wheel band saws because they can cause a lot of trouble. The wheels are so small that the blade overflexes—causing it to crack and finally break—unless you buy the extra thin blades, which are extra flimsy and hard to find.

If your band saw is not equipped for more than a single-speed operation, it may be possible to modify it to run at any of several speeds. One easy way to do this is to mount the motor on a hinge directly below the saw, like the one in the drawing on page 23. Put a three- or four-size cluster pulley in place of the single V-belt pulley. The weight of the motor furnishes the belt tension and you can change saw speeds in seconds. (Refer to section on Variable Speed Machines, p. 22.)

A ⅓-horsepower motor can get you by on a small band saw if you don't push it.

Electric Kiln

This is an oblong metal box lined with soft fire bricks and heated by one or more electrical elements. Such a device heats the blade evenly and completely

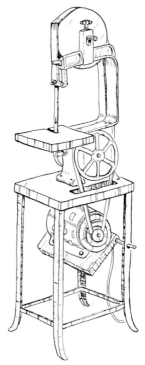

Two-wheel band saw

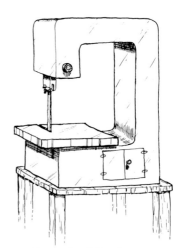

Four-wheel band saw

while giving off virtually no fumes to impregnate the surface of the steel. A small gas-powered kiln could perhaps do as well, but I have never used one. I started with an old top-loading ceramics kiln, then designed and built one just for hardening knives. Once it is heated fully, it should be capable of bringing the knife (or knives) up to temperature in five to fifteen minutes and should allow handy placement and removal of knives.

Use notched soft fire bricks as racks to hold the knives upright in the kiln. Place the blades in the rack edge upwards for even distribution of the heat. This is one piece of equipment that is optional, since some very advanced knifemakers manage to harden with an oxyacetylene torch or a coal-burning forge. I would suppose, however, that the kiln is preferable for most production work requiring very even heating temperatures, such as that needed for the long slender knives used for boning and fileting. The proper kiln is very easy and clean to use and does a perfect job every time.

A temperature gauge and a thermostat are very handy to have on a kiln. If the kiln that you have is not equipped with these devices, you can add them quite easily. The "temperature gauge" is really a *thermocouple* which is connected to a millivoltmeter, which reads the electric charge generated by the heated tip of the thermocouple, and the millivolts appear as degrees of heat on the gauge dial.

The automatic temperature control mechanism is installed between the incoming hot wires and the kiln elements. This switch is designed to maintain a certain set temperature inside the kiln. See your local ceramics supply dealer for any and all things related to kilns. You might decide to build one specially shaped just to hold knives.

I have two small electric kilns—one for preheat-

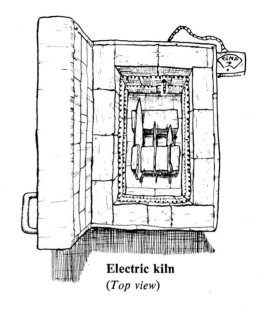

Electric kiln
(*Top view*)

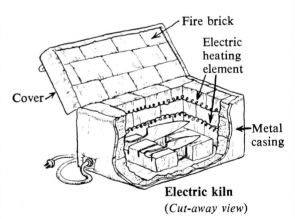

Fire brick

Electric heating element

Cover

Metal casing

Electric kiln
(*Cut-away view*)

ing alloy steels prior to the hardening step, and the other to bring the blades to the proper hardening temperature. (See the appendix, Introduction to Alloy Steels.)

Forge

This could be used to temper the blades in place of the kiln if a heating box is constructed out of fire bricks to focus and distribute the heat along the length of the knife shank. Set the knife in the coals on edge, with the cutting edge directed upward so it will be heated evenly.

A forge will also be of some use should you decide to use forge-hammering as a means of shaping and hardening the blades. These techniques are not covered in this book, however.

Anvil

A good flat anvil is essential for straightening the blades. It can be made out of a railroad track if necessary. The anvil surface should have a slightly concave area, also referred to as a very shallow "mold," which can be used for straightening blades with minimal hammer force. You can grind a shallow impression into the face of an anvil or railroad track with the belt sander or grinder. Make the impression come right up to the square end or edge of the anvil so you can attack kinks right up the handle or bolster area.

Micrometer

I find a 1-inch micrometer invaluable in knife-making. It enables me to tell the exact thickness of a piece of steel, and, more important, the thickness and evenness of my ground edges. Without a micrometer, gauging the thickness of the edge is just guesswork. You will hit it right sometimes, and other times the blade will be too thin, thick, or uneven.

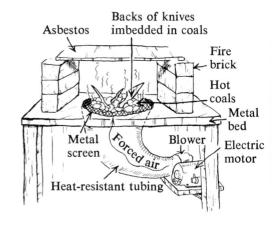

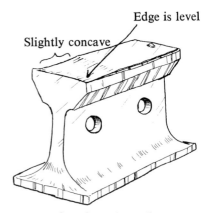

Railroad-track anvil

Small Tools

You need lots of other tools, some for working on knives and some to keep your shop running smoothly. These would include a pair each of blacksmith tongs, pliers, and Vise Grips, a vise, a propane torch, a small bench grinder, a heavy hammer, some files and C clamps, a buffing wheel, a set of open-end wrenches for working on machines. Again, I suggest you check with the local flea market or junk dealer to get yourself a smattering of the basic tools if you don't already have them.

If you are going to do some knifemaking, patience and ingenuity are as important as inspiration and resolve. Don't burn yourself out by trying the actual knifemaking before you are ready. Prepare yourself as best you can, and take your time about it. The quality of your knives will reflect the way you went about making them. Spend your evenings paging through tool-making and metallurgy books. Take good care of your tools and plan your shop arrangement, making it neat, with a place for each thing.

Arranging the Shop

I arrange things so my tools are all in a tight little row with a high spacious workbench just opposite them. This allows me to turn around from any tool and be practically at the workbench.

All the small tools go in a set of drawers right under the workbench. There is a low, strong table right next to the belt sander to pile the belts on and do odd jobs. It is also used for riveting and welding. It has a piece of railroad track and a hand-operated punch press bolted to it. I use the punch press for putting slots in metal pieces for hilts and finger guards. Then, off to the side and out of the way of my regular knifemaking area is a circular saw and a joiner (wood planer). I use these tools to mill down larger pieces of wood for knife handles. Having all these tools set up this way comes in very handy for doing many other things besides knifemaking.

Lighting

You may find, as I have, that fluorescent lights are far more efficient and provide better area illumination than do incandescent bulbs. Use the incandescents to spotlight the working area of each machine. Fluorescent light fixtures are fairly easy to find in swap meets and second-hand stores that specialize in interior fixtures.

Chapter 3

Different Kinds of Knives

We have one more area to cover before we actually start making knives—kinds of knives. You can be thinking about this while you are getting your shop ready. I will present some of the more common types of knives and try to point out how their shape helps convey the desired kind of energy from the hand to

Vegetable knives of the French chef's design.

the work. By and large, I have come to respect these shapes as useful, beautiful, and salable. These are designs that many people can relate to, with specific grinding instructions for each kind of knife. If you get confused, read the sections on grinding and tempering first, then read this chapter.

Vegetable Knife

The French chef's knife has a long, gently curving blade. The curve is usually more pronounced near the tip. The dropped edge gives good finger clearance for chopping and dicing vegetables by rapidly rocking the knife up and down along its edge.

This is a very old and popular design and every kitchen should have at least one, or perhaps a long one and a short one. Blade length can run from 5 to 12

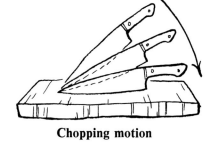

Chopping motion

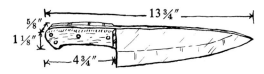

French chef's knife

inches or more. A good size for the home kitchen is about 8 inches. The dropped edge can be from 1 inch to about 2½ inches below the handle.

The handle of a chef's knife, as well as all chopping and carving knife handles, should be large enough to accommodate the full grasp of a closed hand.

The blade has a high, fine, hollow grind, or a fine wedge shape. The first ½ inch or so of steel above the cutting edge should be as thin and strong as possible for minimum cutting resistance, as well as ease of sharpening. If it is finely ground up to ½ inch, it will

Cross section

take an easy edge, even after many years of sharpening. It is best to first grind to only a moderately thin edge, then temper, and complete the grinding of the very fine edge on a belt grinder or a water-cooled grinder. I have warped more chef's knives in the tempering process than I care to think about.

When grinding a very fine edge, check it often so that it doesn't get too thin in one spot—remember, thin steel heats up very fast and won't re-temper—so, constantly dip the blade in water and run your finger along the edge to make sure the grinding is even. Use bare hands, not gloves, to grind a blade after tempering, so you can feel the heat of the blade.

Filet Knives

Filet knives should be fairly long (5 inches to 12 inches) and very thin, narrow, and flexible. You can

Filet knives. The smallest one is for trout, or perhaps eggplant. *Etchings by Francine Martin.*

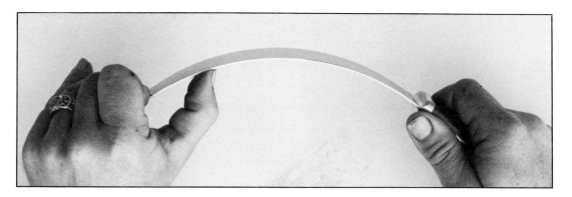

An example of the flexibility of a good filet knife.

grind this blade much thinner without warping during the tempering process because the entire blade is thin. Whereas, with a hollow-ground chef's knife, the back of the blade is thicker for strength and weight. Hence, the different cooling speeds of the different thicknesses can cause warpage in thin areas of the vegetable knife. (See tempering section, p. 116.)

The widths of filet knives range from ¼ inch on narrow, short-bladed knives to 1 inch or so on the longer ones. Since their function is slicing thin slabs of meat along the contour of a bony area, such as fileting meat off the ribcage of a fish, the filet knife needs flexibility.

Use very thin steel and grind to a very fine wedge shape. A hollow grind is very awkward on a narrow blade and serves no purpose. After grinding the edge by about 50 percent, slip the long blade of the filet knife between the wheel and work rest, running it from one end of the blade to the other. Bending the handle towards you, pry the blade into the wheel. This twists the blade so the area along the cutting edge has good steady pressure against the stone; otherwise, the extreme flexibility of the thin steel makes it hard to apply pressure with only the hands.

After grinding, the blade is finished on the belt

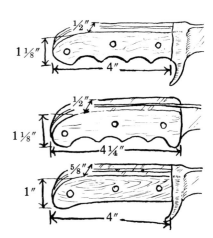

Handle styles for filet knives

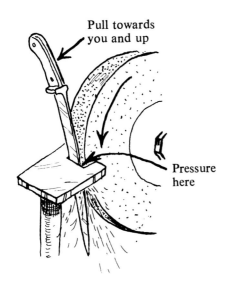

Pull towards you and up

Pressure here

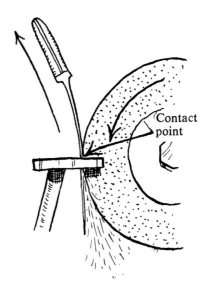

Contact point

machine like all wedge blades, by running the blade up and down the wheel in line with the belt.

A filet knife should have either a guard, finger grips, or simply a thick area in the handle near the blade.

The Butcher Knife

This heavy-duty meat knife is used for butchering large hunks of meat, cutting joints apart, slicing steaks, chopping gristle, et cetera. Its blade is usually fairly straight with a curved end.

The blade, which is 1 or 1½ inches in width and 6 to 10 or more inches in length, is made with medium-thick steel (⅛ inch thick). It is not hollow ground, but has a fairly fine convex bevel. The butcher knife's weight ranges from medium-light to a very heavy bone cruncher, with the grinding varying considerably, too, from a fine straight bevel to a blunt clear-edge convex bevel.

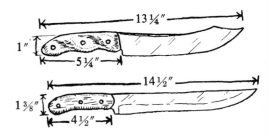

13 ¼″

1″

5 ¼″

14½″

1 ⅜″

4½″

Butcher knives

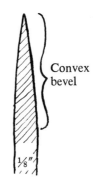

Convex bevel

⅛″

Cross section

45

Carving knives.
Etchings by Francine Martin.

Carving Knife

More slender and graceful than the butcher knife, with a more pointed tip, the carving knife is also quite rigid. The steel thickness is the same ⅛ inch.

Traditionally, carving knives are fancy with a finger guard and a bone handle. They can be either hollow ground or a straight bevel. This knife is about half-way between a curved filet knife and a butcher knife.

Carving Fork

The fork is usually made from the same steel and the same handle material as the knife. Cut the tines with the torch, grind down and polish, then heat to a dull red with the welding tip, and bend the heated area near the tines as shown.

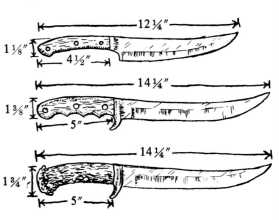

Carving knives

Using a free area of the abrasive belt, i.e. some place away from the wheel, grind between the tines. If you do not have such a free space on your machine, or if you are working without a belt grinder, use a file and pieces of abrasive glued to a thin board.

The shape of the handle should be comfortable for either holding upside down or right side up, because it is held in either position in carving.

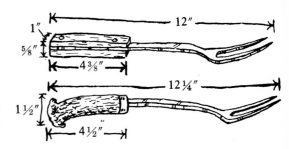

Carving forks

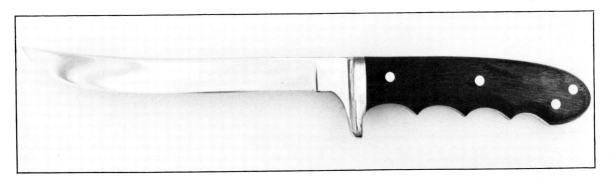

A boning knife.

Boning Knife

This knife is long and slender for cutting meat away from the bone, but it is more rigid than a filet knife. The blade is bent back from the line of the handle so the force of the arm pushes down harder on the blade at the curved end, giving more pressure and thus less tendency for the hand to slip forward. Many are made "backwards," with the cutting edge opposite the finger grips for cutting upwards. These knives look like they are sharpened down to almost nothing, even when new, because of the shape of the cutting edge.

Chopping Knives

Also called Chinese chopping knives, they are used to chop piles of food in single downward strokes of their straight blade, or the blade is pivoted on the

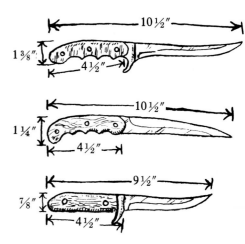

Boning knives

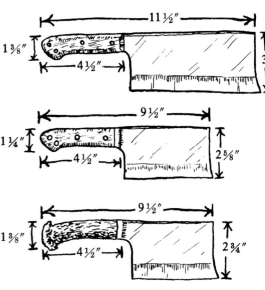

Chopping knives

Chopping knives.
Etchings by Francine Martin.

Chopping motion

base edge and moved in an awkward, but effective, chopping action across the food.

The square shape provides plenty of weight along the whole length of the blade. Oriental cooks use them for very precise, high-speed chopping. While one hand is chopping, the other hand is feeding in the vegetables and guiding the path of the blade.

Blade grinding is identical to that used for the French chef's blade.

This is a chopping knife designed to be used in a wooden bowl.

Bread Knives

Bread knives should have a fine edge, thin shank, and enough length to comfortably slice a loaf. Small notches can be cut into the edge with a $1/32$-inch cutoff wheel to produce a sawtooth blade for cutting hard crust. Bread knives are often used to make sandwiches, so it is functional to have a fairly blunt, broad end for spreading mayonnaise, butter, etc.

A knife like this can become a utility kitchen knife, serving as a spatula if it is wide enough. Al-

though a little unorthodox, a short sandwich knife with a square tip about 2 inches wide, made of very thin, flexible steel, can serve as a spatula and a bread-sandwich knife.

Bread knives. If a straight bread knife were to be made a little heavier and perhaps a little longer, it would be a first-class slicing knife.

Etchings by Francine Martin.

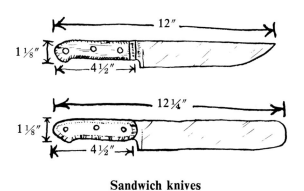

Sandwich knives

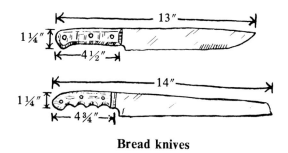

Bread knives

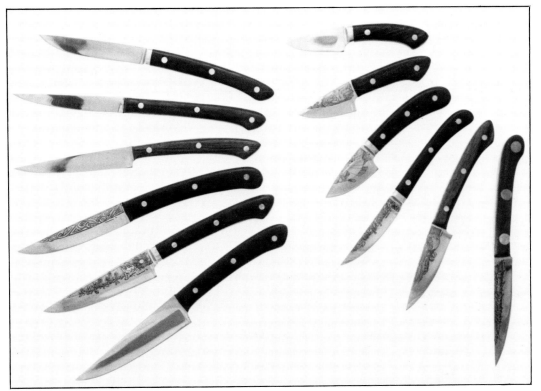

Paring Knives

The paring blade, usually very slender, is anywhere from 1 to 5 inches long. A kitchen needs several with different length blades. The longer ones are used for slicing, peeling, and fileting, and the shorter blades are used at the tip, for cleaning potatoes, et cetera.

Make a fairly fine edge on paring knives. Drop the edge down about a ½ inch or so for cutting on a board. A paring knife is really a light-duty utility knife. The shapes of the ones I make are shown.

Meat Cleavers

Meat cleavers are made from heavy steel. Circular saw blades are a good source for this thick steel,

Paring knives.

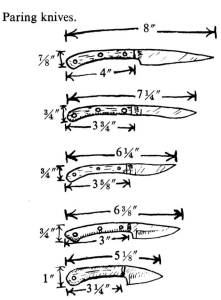

Paring knives

which ranges up to ¼-inch thick. The shape is different from that of a vegetable chopper; it should be thicker, wider, generally shorter, and with a curved cutting edge. The cutting edge should be a thick, convex wedge, like a light hatchet edge. (See chapter 5, p. 69.)

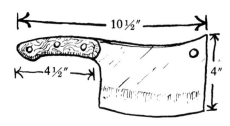

Meat cleaver

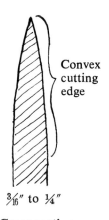

Convex cutting edge

³⁄₁₆″ to ¼″

Cross section

Skinning knives.
Etchings by Francine Martin.

Skinning Knives

The traditional skinning knife has a curved blade from 1 to 8 inches long. It usually has a finger guard or a molded handle that keeps blood and grease off the hand when gutting or skinning an animal.

The skinning knife's blade is curved to expose the edge for scraping the hide bare. Most skinners are particularly curved near the tip for working the hide away from fat and gristle. A "bull-nosed skinner" has no tip at all. Its cutting edge curves completely around a broad, blunt end and goes an inch or more up the back of the knife.

Naturally, you'll design your skinning knife for the kind of work you have in store for it. In fact, many skinning knives are utility knives with a short, curved blade and finger guard. If the blade's curve is not too radical, it serves to clean and butcher game, as well as prepare food. In short, it makes a very practical camp knife.

Many respected knifemakers recommend skinning and utility knives which are much shorter in the blade, and lighter, than the old-time knives. Some of the shapes that are strictly for skinning and cleaning game are shown.

Grind the edge fine, but not flimsy—remember, the finer you grind, the better it will cut but the weaker it will be. If you plan to use the knife for heavy work, do not make it too thin. The grind and the thickness are totally an individual matter with skinning knives.

Utility Knife

A utility knife is a multipurpose knife. This knife is handy for many uses: food preparation, from cleaning fish, skinning and cleaning game to slicing cheese or stripping bark; a knife to take backpacking, one that is strong and light; and a handy knife that will whittle and trim.

An assortment of utility knives' shapes that have been in common use is shown.

I have found these knives, which are prototypes for most knives in common usage, to be overly large

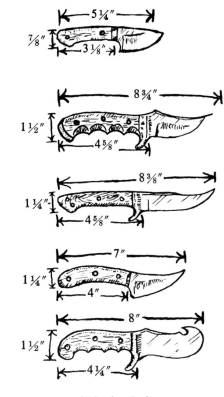

Skinning knives

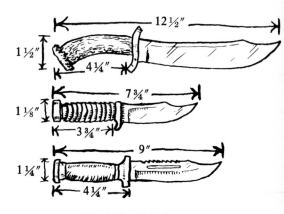

Traditional knives

and clumsy. The handles are not fitted to the hand, and the blades do not flow gracefully from the handle.

Utility and "side" knives have become considerably smaller over the years. Back in Jim Bowie's time, one didn't need a great imagination to picture himself hewing timber for shelter, or fighting

Utility knives. Note that the blade area near the tip is a little straighter on the utility knives than on the skinning knives.
Etchings by Francine Martin.

for his life with a bear. The romance of the mountain men and their real need for large, heavy knives helped prolong the popularity of the "big knife" well beyond its practicality. Many of the early knives were actually short, heavy swords. Knives people use today have become much smaller and lighter because they are easier to carry and control.

The general utility knife should be a short, slightly curved blade with the cutting edge dropped slightly below the handle, forming a natural finger guard and leaving some room for the fingers between the handle and cutting board.

This dropped edge enhances the effectiveness of the knife in preparing food because you can cut meat and vegetables in the middle of a cutting board instead of along the edge, as you would have to with a built-on finger guard.

The dropped blade is also good for butchering and skinning because you have the protection of the natural finger guard with no bulky, manufactured guard getting in the way of the cutting action. Since the edge is below the fingers, they stay cleaner and less slippery. A 2½-inch (or less) utility blade is adequate for most hunting and camping functions, including food preparation. The steel for a knife like this can vary, but need be only ⅛-inch thick or less to provide plenty of strength and heft.

Another very useful feature in a utility knife is a slight curve to the handle, making it conform to the hand. It's even better to have a little bump or hook at the end of the handle for the little finger to push against.

A number of possible shapes for utility knives that are more practical than the larger, traditional utility knives are shown.

Grinding techniques for utility knife blades can vary as much as the shapes. In general, you don't want an edge to be too thin if the knife is for outdoor use.

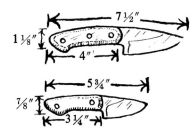

Dropped-edge knives

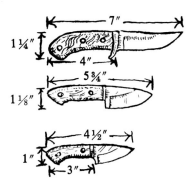

Utility knives

Hatchet

Following ordinary knifemaking procedures, you can turn large heavy circular-saw blades into fine hatchets. A hatchet tends to be heavy unless you use a light piece of steel, say ⅛-inch thick.

The chopping action is a little different from that of an ordinary wooden-handled hatchet, which has the center of balance closer to the head. The full-tang hatchet is highly prized among hunters and collectors because it is solid and packs a good wallop. This tool is similar to a cleaver, but with a short blade and long, gracefully curving handle.

The edge is a convex bevel. You can grind it as fine or as blunt as you wish, depending on what you want to use it for. If it is too fine, the edge may chip in heavy use; if it is too blunt, it may dull easily, not bite as deeply, and become difficult to sharpen. A good compromise edge for a hatchet is shown.

Different Types of Handles

There are two basic kinds of knife handles: *scale*, or *slab*, handles, where two pieces of wood or other material sandwich the tang; and *one-piece* handles, where the tang disappears within the handle.

With either of these, the tang may or may not run the full length of the handle. The *half-tang handle* usually consists of a single piece of handle material notched out to receive the partial tang, although sometimes you will see a partial-tang scale handle.

While full-tang handles tend to be stronger, the quality, effectiveness, and beauty of the handle depends not so much on which type it is, but on how well it is made and the quality of materials. When properly constructed and cared for, the partial-tang handles can last a lifetime or more. However, aside from at least a theoretical, if not mechanical disadvantage, the popularity of a partial-tang handle suffers

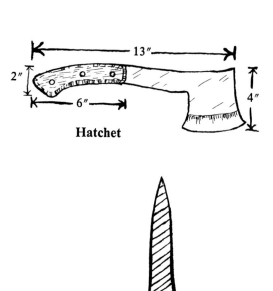

Hatchet

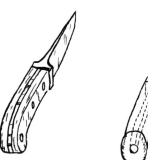

Slab or scale handle (*Full-tang*)

One-piece handle with tang imbedded in handle

A variety of full-tang scale handles.

from a psychological disadvantage—that is, some people like to see the full tang. *You can never really know* how strong a handle is merely by looking at it unless you can see how much of the shank you have a hold on, and how it is connected. Since many of the partial-tang knives have a tendency to break, people tend not to trust them.

Obviously, there is a wide range of ways to construct knife handles. This is one of the factors that make bench-made knives unique—the variety of handle types. In this book, I am going to describe two major methods of handle construction: the *full-tang scale handle* and the *half-tang one-piece handle*. These simple-to-make handles can be durable and beautiful. If you make knives with one or both of these methods, and then wish to devise some other method, it will not be difficult, because you will have penetrated the "sense" of the problem.

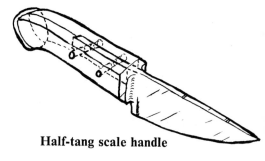

Half-tang scale handle

Designing the Knife

Now that you know what kind of knife you want, draw a full-scale outline on a piece of cardboard or posterboard. After you feel satisfied with the silhouette, cut it out with a razor knife or band saw. Pretend it is a real knife. How does it feel? Keep it around for a day or two and see how your feelings change about the shape. You may redesign the knife several times while it is still in the cardboard state. This cardboard shape will be used as a template to trace the outline onto the steel.

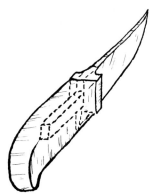

Half-tang one-piece handle

Designing the Handle

As you design your knife, consider the type of handle it will have. If it is a full-tang scale handle, the silhouette of the tang is, of course, the same as the silhouette of the entire handle.

The one-piece *partial* tang can be drawn out in the following way. Draw the outline of the entire knife on cardboard. Try out the design as described above and refine the shape until you are satisfied. Now, on the cardboard silhouette, outline the area that will be made of steel, including the tang.

This will be the template with which you will trace the outline onto the steel.

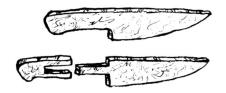

Cardboard

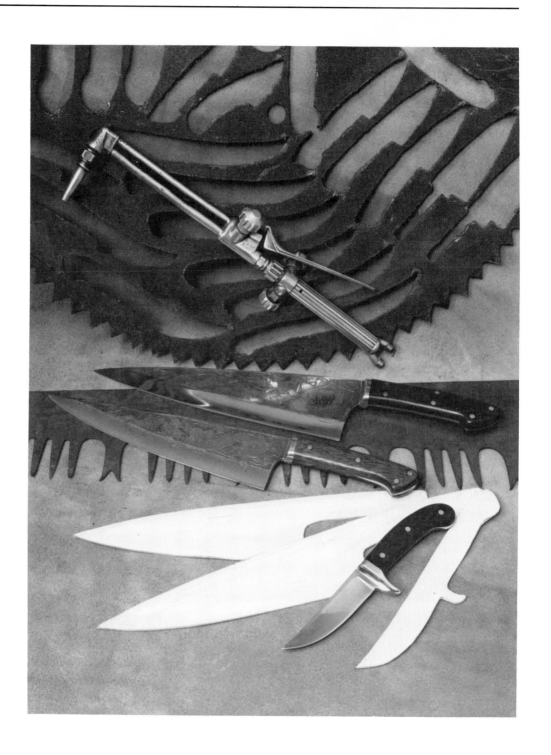

Chapter 4

Cutting Out the Blade

Assuming you have chosen your knife's function, have designed it, and chosen the steel, you are ready to cut out the rough shape.

Use a cutting torch or a band saw. The cutting torch leaves jagged edges, so a lot of grinding is needed to smooth them and to refine the silhouette. Moreover, if the steel is not properly annealed, the concentrated heat from the torch can cause stress lines (lines of weakness that you cannot see) that will later become cracks. But the torch works fine for carbon steel, and it may be more accessible than a band saw that can cut hard steel. Furthermore, you may find a cutting torch faster than a band saw for production knife work, especially if you are cutting knives from large pieces of stock. I have had very good results using the cutting torch for production work with carbon steel saw-blade stock. Let's assume, therefore, you will use a cutting torch. (See section on band saws in "Tools", chapter 2, p. 34.)

Drawing the Knife onto the Steel

First, clean the steel thoroughly. If, in fact, you are using an old saw blade, grind the rust off with a disc grinder, or sandpaper by hand if necessary.

Next, draw the silhouette of the knife. If you are using a cutting torch to cut it out, make the line about ⅛-inch larger in all directions than you want the finished silhouette to be, to accommodate for the

I get a little tense when giving birth to a blade.

clean-up grinding. Use chalk, soapstone, marking pen, or what have you, to draw out the design. I have not found a marker that will show up on all kinds of surfaces (for example, smooth *and* pitted), therefore, I sometimes smoke the surface of the steel with a low acetylene flame until thoroughly blackened, then draw out the shapes with a pointed stick.

If the knife has a molded grip (finger grips in the handle), do not draw the grips onto the steel but leave room for them so they can be ground in later. Do not draw in the finger guard either, since this will be made of brass.

If you are making a number of knives, save steel by drawing them as close to each other as you can. Make the edges run longitudinally with the piece of steel, because this is most likely the direction of the grain inside the steel.

If you are recycling used steel, be sure to check for any cracks that may have formed in its past life.

Grinding heavy rust off a saw blade.

Cutting out some utility sheath blanks with a torch.

Cutting the Steel with a Torch

If you use an acetylene torch, draw out a number of shapes on the same piece of flat stock and cut them all out in one operation. If you are using a band saw, it is better to reduce the size of the stock to only slightly larger than the intended knife blade. The acetylene torch is probably faster in cutting out a number of knives from a large piece of steel, but affords less control when it comes to the precise contours of the blade.

Here are some ways to improve the efficiency and precision of the cutting torch performance:

1. Thoroughly clean the steel before cutting.
2. Use a small-size tip; keep it clean.
3. Use an open metal frame to support the stock while cutting.
4. Thoroughly preheat when starting a cut before shooting oxygen or you may "blow away" part of the knife.
5. Do not have the oxygen pressure too high or it will pop. If the little beads of molten steel

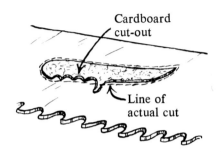

Knife shapes outlined on saw

Cutting a utility sheath knife from A2 steel with a band saw.

which roll away from the flame on the top of the steel become superheated and explode, increase acetylene pressure or decrease oxygen pressure at the tank regulator.

6. If using a wide piece of stock, start with the shapes farthest away and work toward yourself, or you will be cooking your hands over hot steel.

Cutting the Steel with a Band Saw

Although this is a slower and more difficult method of cutting out the blade, it is superior because it is much more precise, and there is very little heat generated which could set up unnecessary stresses in the steel.

To keep from ruining any steel-cutting band saw blade, the first rule is that the steel that you cut must be properly annealed. If you buy from the factory, the steel will most likely be in the annealed state when you get it. If not, then you can't cut it with a band saw unless you anneal the steel yourself.

To anneal saw-blade steel, or any low-alloy carbon steel, heat it in a kiln to about 1,200°F. (dull, faint red) and cool slowly for three hours by turning the kiln off with the steel still inside. Or, heat the blade and place it in powdered lime or fireplace ashes to hold the heat in the steel, causing it to cool very slowly.

The metal-cutting blade must be of fine quality, and with teeth small enough so that three are on the workpiece at all times. So, for ⅜-inch steel, you should use an eighteen-tooth-per-inch blade.

It is also important that the saw runs at the right speed. Unfortunately, for cutting steel, the right speed is very, very slow. Around 80 FPM for most steel-cutting blades. I had to modify my saw with a double set of large and small pulleys to make it run slowly enough so that it didn't knock the teeth off the blade.

Usually, if I have a number of knives to complete, I perform each step on all the knives in the following order: cut them all out, clean the silhouettes, then grind all the edges, et cetera. (See chapter 18, p. 203.)

If you cut out the knife with a torch, the subtle aspects of the form are shaped on the grinding wheel. If you use a band saw, the design can be more nearly perfected during the process of drawing (or tracing) it onto the steel. In either case, you will likely be refining the shape with the wheel.

Refining the Shape

A knife has movement even when it is lying on the table. This movement is the total interplay of the forces of the lines that describe it. So you must ask yourself what will the knife be used for? You must

Refining the shape of a chopping knife with a heavy grindstone.

generate a subtle feeling that is the soul-birth of the knife and translate this feeling into the outline of the knife. The reader must understand that I am not trying to be poetic here; this is an actual knifemaking process or technique—the subtle transfer of the inner impulse of the knife from inside yourself out to the physical world in the form of the knife. It is one of the absolutely crucial elements in successful knifemaking.

First, grind off all rough torch marks, if any, from around the edge, leaving a completely clean and square edge around the entire knife. Grind in the finger grips if the knife is to have a molded handle. First, draw them in pencil, and then grind away the unwanted steel, using an overlapped rough abrasive belt on the belt grinder.

Cutting finger grips

Hold the knife and pretend to be using it. Swing it through the air with the movement for which it is being designed. If it is a carving knife, carve an imaginary turkey. Then, look at the shape. Is it graceful? Is it natural for those movements? Do the lines of force extending from your arm and hand follow directly to where the cutting edge meets the turkey? Is the action of the cutting movement a single line of force extending through the body and out the cutting edge and into the object being cut? Is it balanced? A balanced knife has a handle that is the proper length and thickness for a given blade and usage. The knife should have a balanced feel in the hand, however, the center of balance is not at any particular point. When a knife is right, you feel the impulse of action move from your center of balance in the abdomen and move right out through your arm straight into the thing you are cutting. This is very subtle and may require some practice and attention to discover exactly what it is that I am saying. The pressure on the blade is balanced. The blade must be wide enough, thick enough, and properly tapered to extend this impulse of action gracefully, and yet it must not be clumsy, bulky, or flimsy. Working with the grinding wheel, you must trim out only the unnecessary areas of steel stock leaving those structural lines that faithfully convey the action. You will get so that you know just what the knife is saying as definitely as if the lines were drawn in chalk. This is the great advantage in hand-shaping each blade individually—the soul of the knife is developed as a unique expression of yourself, and the real birth of this soul is in the shaping process.

Hold the knife up and examine the silhouette. Run it across the wheel a couple of times, then hold it up again. Carve off another piece of the turkey or chop a few more onions, then trim a little more metal away. Observe the flowing line up the spine from the handle to the tip. Check for the desired finger clearance. Think about any plans for a bronze hilt or butt, and consider any future etching. Picture the line of the handle. Conceive clearly how you will finish the knife. At a certain point, you will know the shape is right. After you have done a number of knives, the shaping process becomes more and more intuitive and correspondingly more graceful and precise.

If you are making a knife for a particular person, picture that person clearly and feel the vibration of that person during the shaping process, as well as during all the other construction steps, and you will help attune the vibration of the knife to the vibration of the person you are making it for.

Straightening the Blade

After you have cut out the knife with the torch and completed the shaping on the grinder, straighten the blade on the anvil. You do not have to get it perfectly straight, but approximately so. It may warp again during the grinding process, and again during the tempering process, and possibly when it is etched. You should straighten the blade whenever heat and pressure cause it to bend. The final straightening operation comes after the heat-treating is completed.

Chapter 5

Grinding the Blade

This is, of course, the essential step in knifemaking. It is also one of the most crucial and difficult. There are a number of different ways to grind a blade, giving it anything from a convex to a concave shape.

Types of Ground Edges

Consider these blade cross-sections and imagine the best uses for each. For example, blade 1, known as a convex bevel, is best for cutting things which are heavy and hard, where a large amount of force is used,

Grinding a small utility knife using a work rest and pressure plate behind the blade. You should first master grinding small knives without the pressure plate behind the blade, because this is trickier than it looks.

such as bone or wood, because the cutting edge is backed by thick, heavy steel which is unlikely to break. Blade 2, known as the concave bevel, is suited to softer materials, such as vegetables or meat where the blade cuts deeply, producing little friction. It's also known as a "hollow" grind because the side of the knife is actually hollowed out along the edge. It cuts more easily, but is not as strong. As the cutting edge wears back after many subsequent sharpenings, the convex blade becomes thicker and thicker, and thus harder and harder to sharpen, while the concave blade stays at about the same thickness for many, many sharpenings.

Blade 3, known as a straight bevel or simple wedge, is half-way between the other two shapes. The intended use of the knife determines the shape and thickness of the cutting edge as well as the way in which it is ground. For 99 percent of my knives, regardless of the ultimate bevel desired, I start out with a hollow grind. If the knife will have a convex bevel, or a straight bevel, then I do not take the hollow grind too deep. I hollow-grind most knives and do about 85 percent of the stock removal with the heavy grindstone. This is a high-speed wheel described in the tool section (See p. 25.)

The Proper Attitude

You can go about this grinding process in two ways: either the intellectual or the intuitive approach. With the intellectual approach, you picture exactly how you want the knife to look and how the grinding will be done.

With the intuitive approach, you get more of a feeling for the knife without many mental pictures, carving metal away until satisfied. Both intelligence and intuition are integral aspects of the knifemaking process.

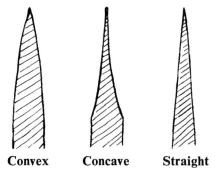

Convex **Concave** **Straight**

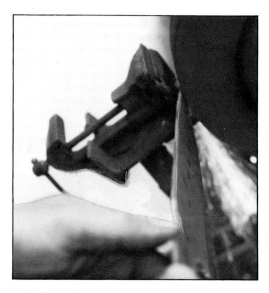

Grinding a long chef's blade using the pressure plate.

Grinding Technique

Begin grinding the blade, taking long, even passes along the full length of the blade. Be careful not to stop in any one place or it will become deeper in that spot. Since this inevitably happens, develop the capacity to feel the evenness of your work so you automatically "lighten up" when you come to a depression or hold longer when you come to a high spot. Grinding, like life itself, becomes self-corrective due to this immediate feedback through the sense of touch—a process of communication. You will notice yourself repeating patterns of stock removal along each blade you grind. Since you have more leverage along the edge nearest the handle, this area may be taken down first, becoming too thin before you realize

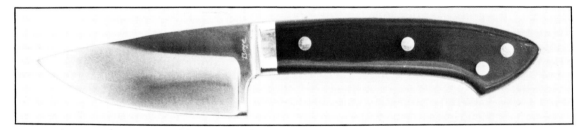

A hollow-ground knife.

You can see from the reflection on the surface that this drop-ped-edge filet knife is flat, rather than hollow, on the sides.

Left side   **Right side**

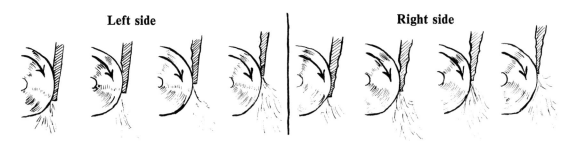

it. Therefore, about half-way through grinding, you should concentrate more intensely to keep the edge even.

The Hollow Grind

Take out a trough along the blade corresponding to the arc of your wheel. Then, tilting the blade backward slightly in subsequent passes, gradually remove more and more stock toward the edge, producing a straight line from the deepest point of the hollow grind to the cutting edge.

Repeat this process until about half the work on one side is finished. Then, turn the blade around and proceed on the other side. The idea is to not take too much off in any one place. When both sides are approximately half-ground, proceed more carefully keeping things even and about the same distance up on each side of the blade. Take your gloves off and dip the blade in water occasionally, running your fingers up and down the edge feeling for thick and thin spots. Grind the blade to about 85 percent of completion, since you will complete the grinding on the belt machine.

If you are grinding a particularly fine (thin) blade, such as a chef's vegetable knife, you may not be able to grind as much prior to tempering. If the blade is ground too thin prior to tempering, it will warp. Therefore, you grind only so thin, temper the blade, then carefully, so as not to heat the blade, regrind it to its desired thickness. This regrinding is best done on a belt grinder, using a fresh, coarse belt, unless you are lucky enough to have a water-cooled grinding wheel or a water-cooled belt grinder, in which case you can use the belts a little longer.

Remember, if you want a smooth job, grind the blade at least three or four more times with the belt grinder, each time with a progressively finer grit belt. Don't grind very deeply with the wheel or it may become too thin for belt grinding. Obviously, how deeply to go each time is a matter of practice.

Grinding the tip of the blade, where the edge tapers off, is difficult; especially getting the hollow grind to go clear to the tip. This means having a very thin tip, but not so thin as to be weak. The line of the hollow grind should be mostly parallel with the edge, but perhaps tapering slightly toward the edge near the tip.

Your eye for a good grinding job improves with practice, with knives you once liked beginning to look clumsy, coarse, or too thin.

The Straight Bevel

Run a series of progressively shallower cuts from the edge up to the backbone of the blade. After you have roughly accomplished a straight bevel in this manner, you have a myriad of shallow grooves running along the knife. Turn the blade 90 degrees so it runs in the same direction as the wheel and grind the blade longitudinally. Use the rest as a fulcrum and lever the blade against the wheel. This removes wheel arcs and saves some work on the belt machine.

The Convex Bevel or Rolled Edge

This is the easiest, or shall I say least exacting, type of blade to make. It is for heavier knives such as cleavers, heavy butcher knives, heavy combat knives, and hatchets. Therefore, there is little danger of accidentally grinding the edge too thin. It is also easier to

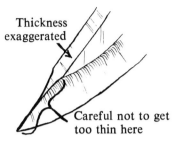

Thickness exaggerated

Careful not to get too thin here

Chef's knife

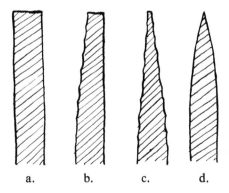

a.   b.   c.   d.

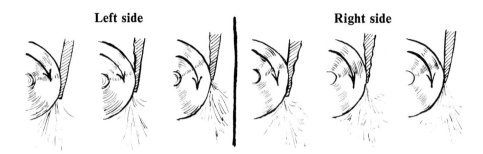

Left side   **Right side**

make the deepest cuts along the edge, where they are easily seen and felt. Simply grind heaviest along the edge, tapering according to the design of the knife.

Finger Guard for Dropped Blade

Whatever the type of blade, grind carefully and evenly. If the dropped blade is to serve as a finger guard, remember to leave unground an ⅛-inch or so on the end of the blade nearest the handle. Make sure this area, where the grinding stops at the base of the blade to form a finger guard, is ground very clearly and sharply. Do not leave the unground finger guard on chef's knives because a finger guard is not necessary, and this thick area will result in an uneven edge after many sharpenings.

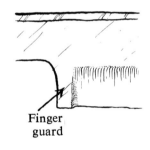

Finger guard

Moreover, be sure the grinding is even on both sides near the handle. Remember, too, that this is the rough-grinding step. If you have a good belt grinder, you will be able to refine the quality and definition of the grinding as well as the surface texture.

After you finish the grinding, sharpen the blade on the grindstone. You will clearly see any bumps and hollows in the grinding. This step saves time on the belt when you sharpen the blade "for keeps." Do not take the blade to a fine edge until much later, or you

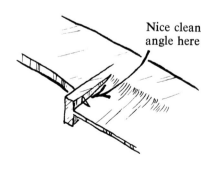

Nice clean angle here

might cut yourself while working on the blade. Later on, when you are more skilled at grinding, you can skip this step, leaving the edge square until the final sharpening (edging) procedure.

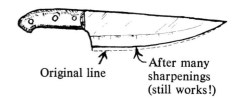

Original line   After many sharpenings (still works!)

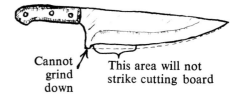

Cannot grind down   This area will not strike cutting board

How Much to Grind Before Heat-treating?

After reading the chapters on regrinding and heat-treating the blade, decide on the desired thickness you want for your blade edge. Consider, too, the best thickness for the blade while it is being treated. You must strike a happy medium between two extremes here: if the blade is too thin when it is heat-treated, it may crack or curl up like a potato chip during the process; if it is too thick when tempered, you will have much more work grinding the steel to its desired thinness. Not only is hardened steel more difficult to grind, but it must be kept cool during the regrinding process.

Some knives have an edge so thick that you could grind them to the final step and then temper, and they would not warp. However, a very thin knife, like a fine chef's blade, would be damaged if it was ground more than 75 percent toward completion.

Take a blade as near to 90 percent of completion as you can, saving about 10 percent of the stock for removal in the regrinding-polishing steps. If it is a very thinly ground edge, especially in relation to the thickness of the back of the blade, remove a smaller percentage of stock before heat-treating. (See chapter 7, p. 105.)

A *micrometer* lessens this problem. Generally I grind the blade to about .03 inch at ¼ inch from the edge before hardening, then grind the blade thinner after tempering, if this is desired. It all depends on the particular blade design, but I find that most of my blades wind up from .024 inch to .028 inch in thickness at ¼ inch from the cutting edge after they have been heat-treated and reground. I have come to favor blades with a fairly fine grind, both for kitchen knives and for outdoor use. The only exceptions are cleavers and heavy butcher knives, and some heavy hunting and survival-type knives.

Now you have an idea of the optimal thinness of the blade edge during heat-treating, right? If so, grind until the blade is *almost* that thin, then use a belt grinder to finish the blade for hardening.

Preparing the Blade for Heat-treating

A fairly smooth surface finish, especially around the perimeter of the blade, is important to keep stresses at a minimum during the heat-treating process. The next operation is to refine the surface of the entire blade, making it smooth and precisely ground.

Regrinding the Blade

Work the blade over the wheel of the belt grinder just as you did with the stone. Remember, if you turn the point or edge of the blade into the belt, the wheel will catch the blade, doing damage to the belt, the blade, and possibly to your hands. Be very careful about this.

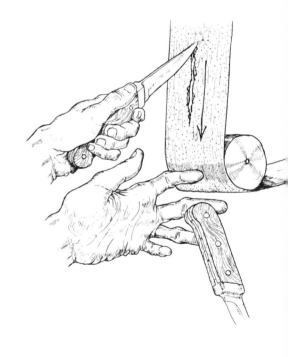

Work with about a 40-grit belt to bring the blade down near to its desired thickness and to take out the marks left from the high-speed grinder, leaving a finer set of 40-grit tracks.

Now, here is one subtle but important point. Be sure to get all of the grinder marks out of the blade because they tend to be deceptively deep. If you do not get them out with the 40-grit belt, they will be even harder to get out when you start working with a finer belt. But, if the grinding marks all run in the same direction, it is hard to see when you have the deeper marks out. You then grind too shallowly, thus leaving in some of the deeper marks to bug you later. If you grind too deeply, you make the blade too thin. You have to discriminate between the 40-grit marks and the grindstone marks that you are trying to remove. To do this, occasionally grind at a slightly different angle until the deeper marks from previous grinding steps are taken out. Change the angle every so often in order to identify the marks that you are grinding away.

Still using the 40-grit belt, remove any undesirable rust pits on the side of the knife and completely refine the shape and contour of the blade.

Now, regrind the blade again, this time using the same method to remove the 40-grit tracks with an 80-grit belt. This is the last full grinding operation prior to tempering (at least for me), so get the knife as near to perfect as you can. When you are done with the 80-grit belt, the blade should look just about finished, except for its rough 80-grit texture.

Before tempering, grind around the silhouette of the entire blade with a 120-grit belt. This finer-textured surface on the edges of the steel minimizes stress during the heat-treating process.

Check the blade for straightness again.

If you plan to braze or weld any additional parts to the knife, now is the time to do it.

**Marks at different angle
are from previous step**

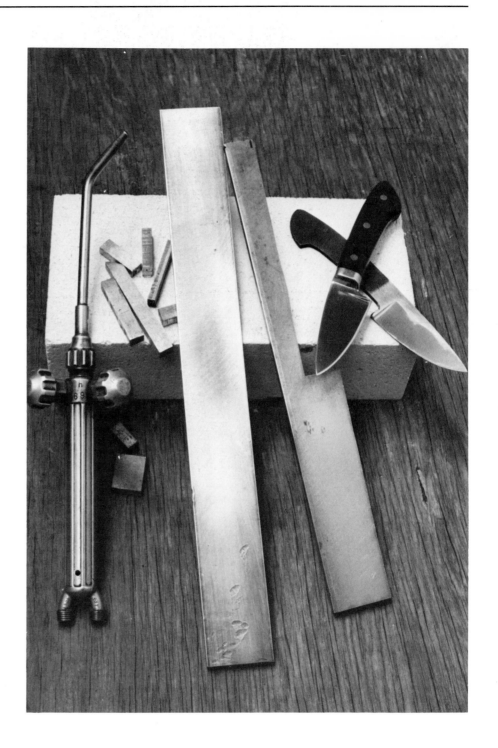

Chapter 6

Building the Bolster, Finger Guard, and Butt Plate

A "bolster" is a piece or pieces of metal joined to the shank between the handle and the blade. This gives the handle material, which is usually soft compared to steel, additional support and protection, and may serve to seal the cracks between the handle and blade. This prevents the intrusion of moisture from food, or possibly blood, which can collect against or underneath the handle.

Sometimes the bolster is extended downward to form a finger guard, or a butt plate may be added to give the handle additional support. The butt may also be extended downward to form a hook for a finger grip.

It is very common to see a handle of some "warm" material such as bone, wood, or plastic, with a brass, stainless, or aluminum bolster and butt.

There are many ways to attach the metal pieces to the shank. The bolster or finger guard may simply be slotted or drilled and slid over the handle or partial tang to rest against stops at the top and bottom of the blade and be held by the pressure of the handle. This arrangement is neither moisture-proof nor very supportive for the handle.

The metals must be tightly and strongly bonded together to make a satisfactory bolster. Three popular

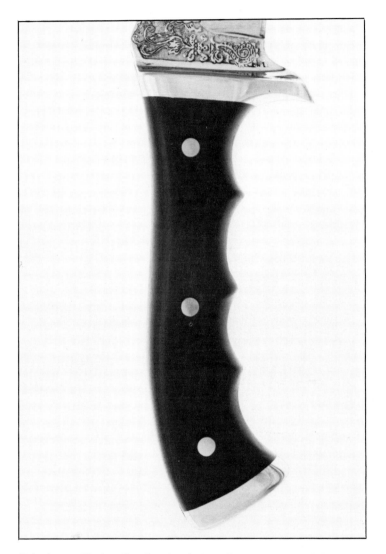

Skinning knife handle showing bolster/finger guard and butt plate.

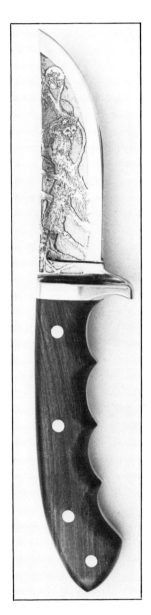

A four-inch skinner with molded grip and bolster/finger guard. *Etching by Jessie Oster.*

ways to do this are to braze the pieces together, solder them, or pin them together. The brazing must be done before hardening, while the soldering and pinning methods are done after tempering. Since I prefer brazing, this is the way I make my knives.

Brazing on the Bolster and/or Butt Cap

"Brazing" is fusing the brass directly onto the steel, forming a very strong and visually pleasing union between the two metals. Braze the bolster prior to tempering because the heat generated ruins any kind of hardness in the carbon steel blade.

Complete the polishing steps up through the 120-grit belt before beginning the brazing process, because the addition of a bolster makes it awkward to polish. The brazing and tempering process will cause scale and discoloration, but the blade will be completely shaped, without any deep grinding marks to remove. However, do not get the blade too thin or it will warp in the quenching bath. If this appears likely, finish the side of the blade with the 120-grit, leaving the ground portion with the 80-grit marks until after tempering.

What Kind of Brass?

Brass can be obtained very reasonably at a good scrap yard or new at a nonferrous metal dealer. Use pieces for brazing that are at least $3/16$ inch or $1/4$ inch thick.

Make sure your brazing brass contains no lead. The brass to use is a mixture of pure copper and zinc. Other types of brass may contain some lead, which will bubble during the brazing process, leaving the work riddled with holes like Swiss cheese. This can be very disturbing, especially if you don't know why ugly holes form in your knife bolster. Although you usually cannot see them until you begin to fair the work down, these holes get bigger and bigger as you try to grind them away.

There is at least one way to test the purity of brass you may buy at a scrap dealer, since the person in charge is unlikely to know the particular quality of a given piece of brass. Use a cutting torch to heat a corner of the brass to the melting point. Pure brass

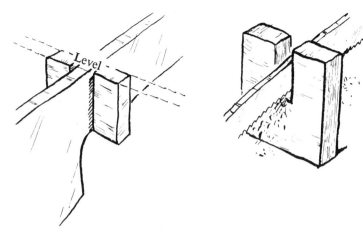

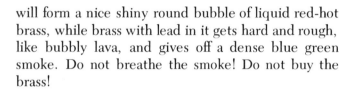

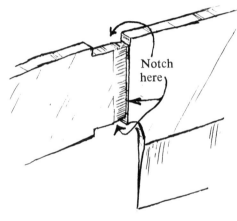

will form a nice shiny round bubble of liquid red-hot brass, while brass with lead in it gets hard and rough, like bubbly lava, and gives off a dense blue green smoke. Do not breathe the smoke! Do not buy the brass!

Bolster Construction for a Full-tang Slab Handle

If you are constructing a plain bolster, cut out two brass "ears" slightly wider than the thickness of the scales, and as long as the width of the knife at that point. I usually use $3/16$-inch or $1/4$-inch brass plate. Square the little pieces off with the belt sander so they fit neatly against the shank.

If you are making a combination bolster and finger guard, use one piece. Cut out a slot down the center line from the top the exact thickness of the blade. Use a hacksaw or the metal-cutting blade of the band saw and a thin flat file to accomplish this.

You can also use the belt sander to grind the inside of the slot to size by sliding the piece over the belt at a point where the belt has no metal backing or wheel directly behind it.

Cut a notch in the edge of the shank at the top and bottom of the bolster using the belt grinder.

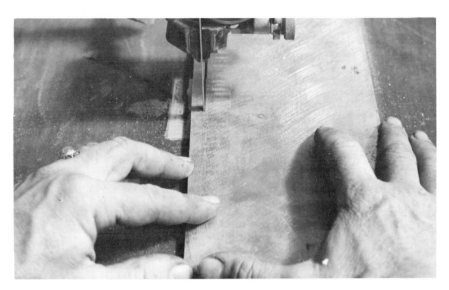

1. Milling ¼-inch brass plate into strips for bolster material.

Make the notches slightly (say ⅛ inch) longer than the thickness of the brass so the built-up areas on the sides will meet the brass fill at the top.

Using the edge of the belt against the flat steel backing plate of the belt grinder, cut another notch along the sides of the blade, joining the front edges of the top and bottom notches.

Make these notches on the side of the shank very clean and sharp. They will be filled with brass during the brazing process, and then the brass will be beveled off flush with the steel right along the notch. The notch makes the fused joint between the brass and the steel perfectly straight and even.

Go over the notches with a file so they are sharp and precise.

During the first brazing step, fill the top notch with brass from the brazing rod. This, in effect, joins the two pieces. When you finish with the brazing, there will be a single brass piece going completely around the shank.

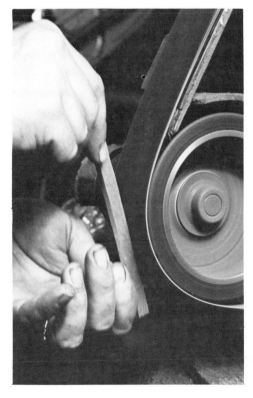

2. Cleaning milled brass strips of bolster material.

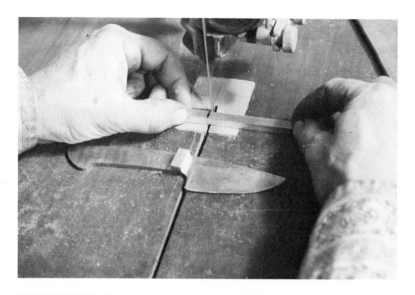

3. Cutting brass ears from milled strip.

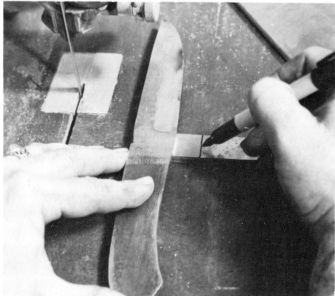

4. Cutting bolster/finger guard from milled stock.

5. Cutting the slot down the center of a prospective bolster/finger guard with a band saw.

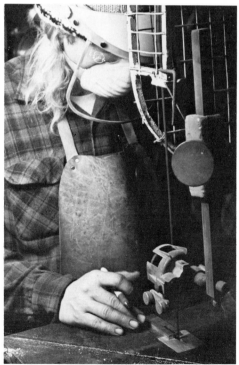

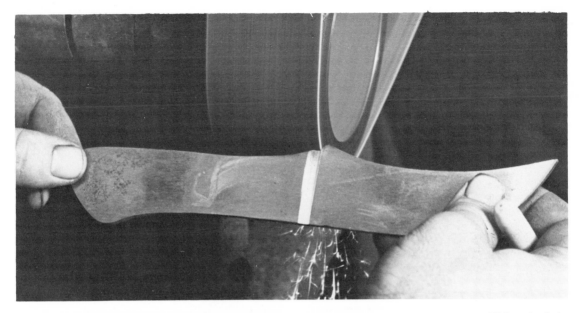

Using the belt grinder to precisely mill out the top notch on a bolster/finger guard. You're right, the edge should be ground before starting the bolster.

Refining the already precise notch which will receive the brass fill, joining the two pieces of brass at the top of the bolster/finger guard.

Grinding the side notches to receive the brass fill. Try this with a file the first few times, because it's trickier than it looks.

Brazing Technique

I recommend powdered rather than liquid brazing flux. You can sprinkle it on and it will stay on the hot workpiece, whereas the liquid just bubbles and flies off.

Use a brazing rod that is approximately ⅛ inch thick. Use a bare rod rather than one that's coated, because with the coated rod, the excess flux piles up

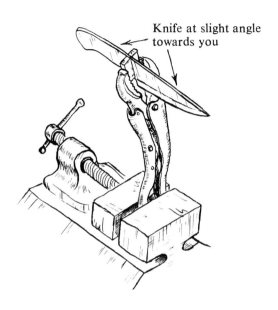

Knife at slight angle towards you

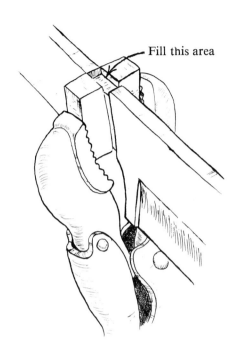

Fill this area

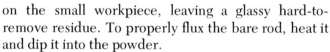

on the small workpiece, leaving a glassy hard-to-remove residue. To properly flux the bare rod, heat it and dip it into the powder.

Clean the brass pieces with a fine, fresh belt.

Clamp the two pieces of brass bolster, or the one-piece bolster/finger guard, to the shank with a pair of Vise Grips, then hold the Vise Grips in a vise so that the workpiece is at a good angle for brazing.

Use a hot flame from a small welding tip and braze across the top of the shank, between the two brass ears. Fill the notch completely, making sure that the rod melts into the brass and flows readily onto the steel.

After this area is filled, remove the hot knife from the Vise Grips and precisely adjust the angle of the "ears," and then form a fine and tight bead around the front side of the bolster, between it and the shank.

Try not to leave any air pockets or cracks. (This operation will obviously require some practice at brazing.) You have to heat the metals right down to the very crack between the brass and steel for the

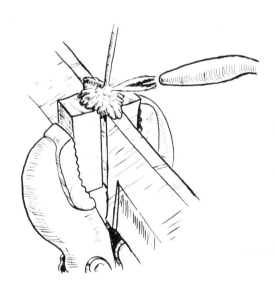

1. Filling the top notch, thus joining the two brass ears of a bolster.

2. Once the two ears have been brazed at the top, check to see if they are precisely straight along the side notches. If not, adjust them by bending them with pliers while still hot.

3. Filling the
notch along the
side of the blade.

4. Filling the
bottom notch.
Remember, you
must get every-
thing thoroughly
heated or you
will uncover cracks
and bubbles when
you fair down.

brazing rod to flow in there. Otherwise, bubbles will appear when you fair down the brazed surface. If this occurs in spite of your efforts, sprinkle on some more flux and try going over the bead again, this time making sure to heat it right down to the very bottom corner of where the two metals come together. Keep the work clean.

Braze the brass point at the bottom edge of the tang, and be sure that the brazing rod flows deeply into the crack at this point.

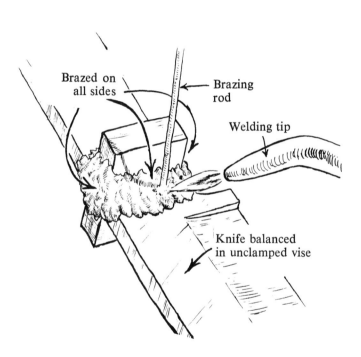
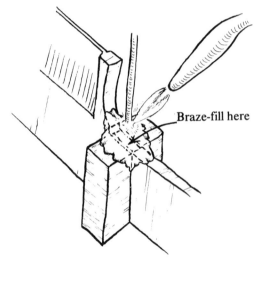

If carbon deposits build up, reducing the brass flow, sprinkle a little powdered flux on the hot workpiece. You will be grinding these areas flush with the handle and you won't want to uncover a crack or a bubble between the brass and the steel.

Do not braze the inside of the bolster where the handle slab butts up against it; instead, leave this area clean and square. Let me repeat this. Do not braze along the inside of the brass where the slab butts up against it, or the joint will look messy and be hard to fit.

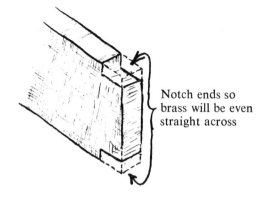

Notch ends so brass will be even straight across

Brazing the Butt Piece

If you are also brazing a butt piece, proceed in the same manner.

Remember to leave the inside surfaces of the brass and the tang nice and clean and square to receive the slabs.

Fairing Down the Bolster

Before tempering the blade, fair down the brass so that it makes a smooth, curved transition to the side of the blade. The brass should meet the steel at the notch on each side of the blade. Use the corner of the belt wheel with the belt overlapped an ⅛ inch to reach this area. Grind the brass enough to see that there are no bubbles or gaps in the brazing, and grind the fill at the top and bottom of the bolster flush with the tang. Proceed to shape the bolster/finger guard.

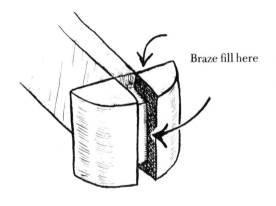

Braze fill here

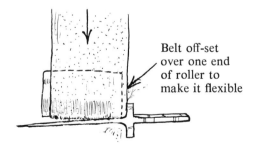

Belt off-set over one end of roller to make it flexible

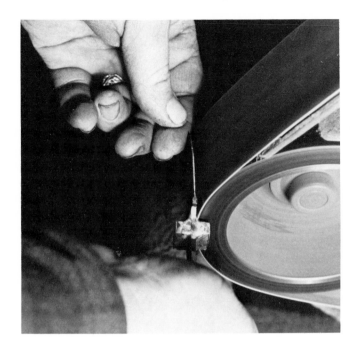

1. Fairing down the fill between the side of the blade and the bolster. It doesn't look like it in the picture, but the stiffness of the edge of the belt has been broken down to produce a rounded fill between the two surfaces.

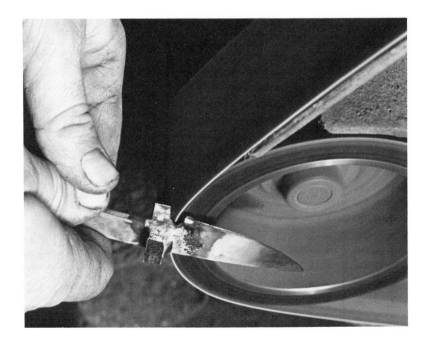

2. Completing the above operation, this time fairing down the fill as it reaches the face of the bolster.

3. Fairing the fill at the top notch flush with the top edge of the tang, all the while hoping not to uncover a bubble.

4. Doing the same at the bottom notch.

 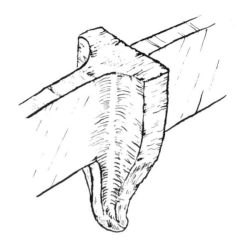

5. Cleaning the area where the dropped blade forms a finger guard.

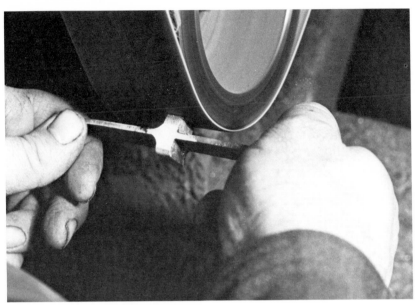

6. Cleaning the sides of the bolster in preparation for hardening. Also, be sure that the sides of the blade have been cleaned up nice and shiny from the brazing process. I have seen some types of acidic brazing flux eat pits in the sides of the blade during the hardening heat-treatment.

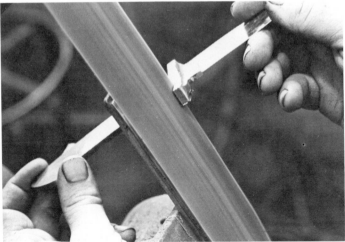

7. Two views showing the finger guard being carved out to fit against the finger, using the softened edge of the belt around the metal edge of the backstop.

Rebraze the piece if you find any insufficiencies. Remember, you cannot rebraze once the blade is tempered, unless you retemper as well.

Removing a Hole

Holes caused by impure brass cannot be repaired without rebrazing in the following manner: First, complete the two remaining steps in the heat-treating process so that the area around the bolster is annealed. Using a small bit that will ream out the hole, drill a small hole straight down through the bubble and into the steel of the knife shank. Drill at least

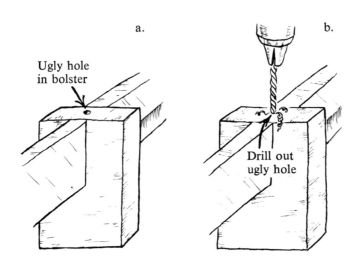

a.

Ugly hole in bolster

b.

Drill out ugly hole

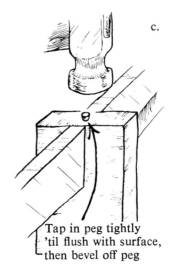

c.

Tap in peg tightly 'til flush with surface, then bevel off peg

three times deeper than the diameter of the hole. You will probably need a cobalt drill bit to penetrate the steel.

Make a clean pin of brass brazing rod to just fit into the hole. Make it slightly longer than the depth of the hole. Holding the bolster securely in the vise, pound the brass pin in until it completely fills the hole. Then, bevel the pin flush with the surface using a fine belt. If you are successful, there should be no trace of the pin or the hole.

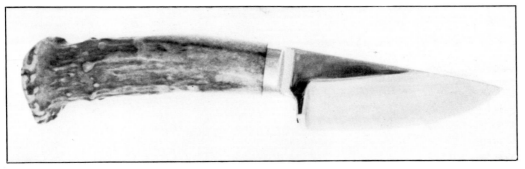

Utility sheath knife with a bolster and one-piece partial-tang handle.

Building a Bolster for a Partial-tang One-piece Handle

Usually this type of handle is made of bone or horn.

If you have designed and shaped the knife properly, there should be a ¼-inch tang extending about 2 inches. You are going to drill a hole in the handle to receive this tang and cement them together with epoxy, right? But you probably want a nice brass bolster, perhaps with a finger guard to butt the handle up against. This brass piece may be brazed on before tempering, or either pinned or soldered on after tempering. It is your choice.

First reread brazing instructions in the preceding section on scale handles. Now, cut the brass out of approximately ¼-inch plate, including the finger guard, if any.

As you do this, hold the blade and handle together and calculate where the handle will butt in and how the handle will look when it's on the tang.

Hold the brass up against the shank and mark where the hole is to be drilled, and drill a 1¼-inch hole in the brass piece. Slide the brass onto the tang. It probably does not go on, so round off the tang a little. Now it fits, but does not snug up against the shoulder of the blade, right? Grind the blade shoulder

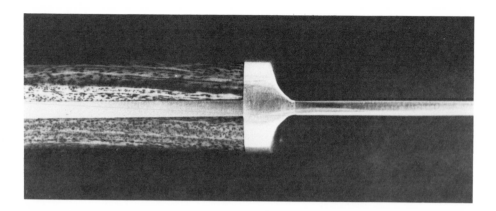

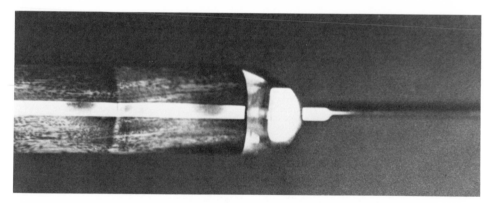

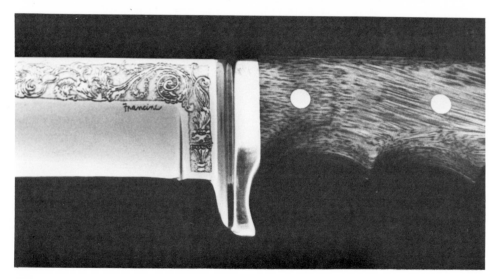

Three views of a finished bolster/finger guard.

a.

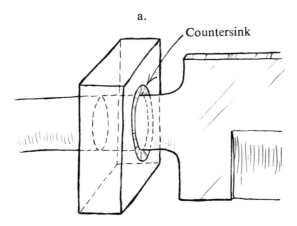

Countersink

b.

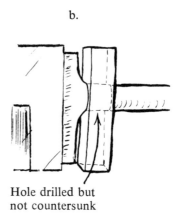

Hole drilled but
not countersunk

nice and square, and ream out the hole in the brass piece with a larger drill bit. Nick off the top and possibly the bottom corner of the blade. This will allow the brazing to be nice and even all the way around.

If the bolster has a finger guard, you do not need a notch at the bottom because the brass is built up in this area. Braze the bolster, filling the area in the front of the bolster, as described in the brazing technique section. Leave the back area unbrazed. Do not worry about the hole in the back of the bolster where the handle butts up, as it will be filled in with epoxy. Fair down and shape the bolster, or bolster/finger guard.

The blade is now ready for tempering. Refer to chapter 14 for instructions on finishing the handle.

c.

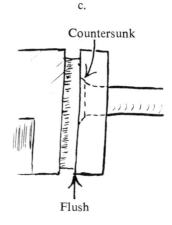

Countersunk

Flush

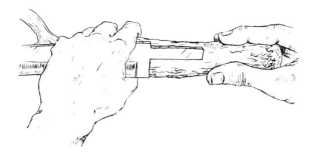

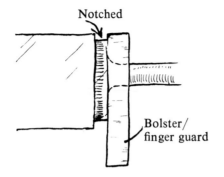

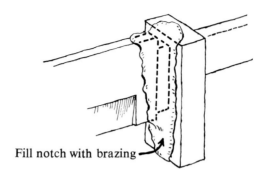

Notched

Bolster/
finger guard

Fill notch with brazing

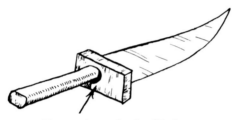

Do not braze back of bolster

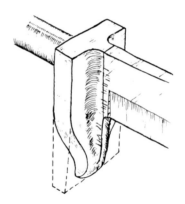

Silver-soldering the Bolster and Butt Cap

Many knifemakers, probably the majority, attach brass or nickel silver pieces to the shank via low-temperature silver solder. This is done *after* the blade has been completely heat-treated and cleaned up. Since solder melts at 450°F., the work can be done with a propane torch, and, if done properly, there is little danger of losing hardness in the steel. Soldering is similar to brazing, except that the solder is not used to fill large areas, but acts as a bond for tightly fitting the pieces of metal. I have not used this method, but I will tell you what I know about it.

Clean the knife and completely clean the brass pieces. Wrap the blade with a wet rag to prevent acci-

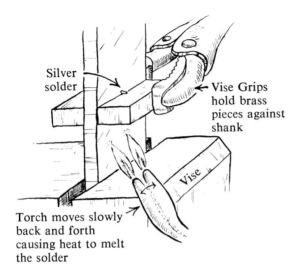

Silver solder

Vise Grips hold brass pieces against shank

Torch moves slowly back and forth causing heat to melt the solder

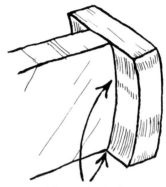

Fits perfectly flush

dental heating and loss of hardness. Place the shank in a vise and clamp the brass piece to the shank in the proper place. As you do this, place a small amount of 450°-silver solder between either the shank and workpiece or at the top on the crack between the pieces. Heat both the shank and the bolster slowly and evenly below the bolster with a very small flame from the welding tip or propane torch until the solder begins to flow. Some flux will aid in this.

If the bolster solder forms a tight little ball and refuses to flow, then either the metal is dirty (contaminated) or you have heated the solder hotter than the workpiece.

The pieces must fit together perfectly so that the solder will flow evenly and form a clean bond. The butt piece, if any, is made and soldered in the same fashion as the bolster.

You should check with someone who has done this operation before trying it yourself, because it is trickier than it seems.

Ready-made Bolster/Finger Guards

Some knifemaker's trade journals offer slotted cast aluminum, brass, and nickel silver bolsters and guards. These pieces are usually joined to the steel shank after tempering with low-temperature silver solder or by pinning.

Connecting the Bolster with Pins

Holes are drilled through the brass and the shank, and pins are driven completely through and peened at each end. Peening the brass rod makes it a little thicker at each end so that it will hold firmly.

Drill the hole the exact size of the rod so it fits snugly. Countersink the holes at each end so that when you peen the ends of the rod, they will expand slightly and become wedged in, completely filling the hole. If this is properly done, you can grind the work flush with virtually no sign of the hole and pin.

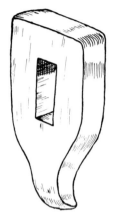

Ready-made bolster

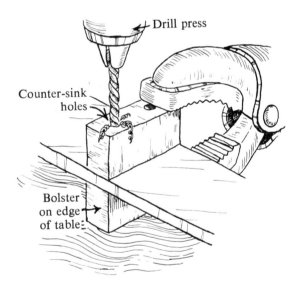

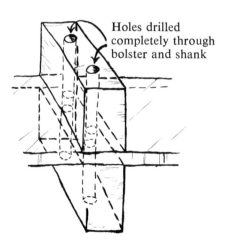

Holes drilled completely through bolster and shank

Holding the pieces together while drilling is difficult. With a pair of Vise Grips turned sideways and shimmed up with a piece of wood, you can drill one hole, set that pin, then turn the knife around in the Vise Grips and drill the other hole.

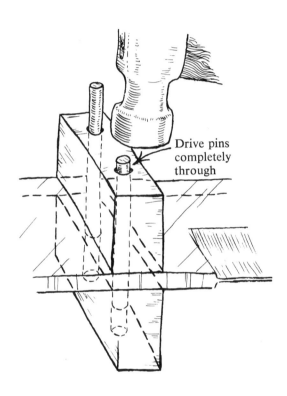

Drive pins completely through

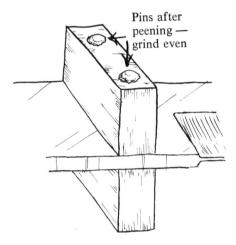

Pins after peening — grind even

Chapter 7

Heat-treating the Carbon Steel Blade*

Techniques for making the steel tough and hard are described in this section. There are three parts to completely heat-treating a carbon steel blade: *hardening*, which is heating the steel to cherry red and quenching in oil or a brine solution; *tempering*, or "drawing," which is taking out the brittleness by slowly heating the steel in an oven until it turns a certain prescribed color; and *annealing* of the tang and backbone of the knife, which is heating these portions of the shank to a deep blue color, followed by slow cooling which makes the steel tough and flexible so the blade cannot snap.

Hardening the Blade

To harden the steel, bring the entire blade to an *even* bright red, or 1,425° to 1,450°F., then plunge it into a quenching bath. Be sure the tongs or rack holding the blade do not cover a crucial edge area; only either the back of the blade or the handle area.

You can use an acetylene torch for medium and small knives, but a small ceramics-type electric kiln is preferable for knives of all sizes. A gas-heated kiln works well if it is large enough to get the knives in and out of. The kiln need only be slightly longer than the

---

* For a more complete discussion of metallurgy theory, as well as practical heat-treatment instructions for several alloy steels popular with advanced knifemakers, see appendix.

length of the knife blade, and only about 4 inches wide for optimal heating speed.

Another possible heating method is to make a long, narrow enclosure over the grate of a forge using a rack to hold the blade upright. If this arrangement is properly done, heating is quick and even, but very critical. Use soft blacksmith's coal as the fuel. (See chapter on Tools, p. 34.)

Whatever heating methods are used, the particular effects of the hardening treatment will be determined by several factors:

1. The *warpage* of the blade will be determined by the evenness with which the heat is applied and the stresses already within the steel.

2. The amount of *discoloration* of the steel's surface will be determined by the purity of the environment when the steel is red hot.

3. The amount of surface *decarburization* will be determined by the time and temperature of the superheated condition.

4. The amount of *internal decay* of the steel will be determined by the time and temperature of the superheated condition.

5. The *hardness* and *toughness* of the steel will be determined by the steel temperature at quenching, the type of bath and its temperature, in addition to the metallurgical characteristics of the steel itself.

Let's discuss each of these factors.

Warpage

Warping occurs when the amount of stress in one area of steel changes in relation to the stress in an adjoining area. If a side of the blade is heated, the molecular tension on that side is relaxed, while the structure on the far side of the blade remains firm, causing the internal structure on the heated side to begin to compress slightly. This will cause the blade to sway away from the heat source. When the steel cools, it retains all or part of this warpage.

I made an electric kiln for tempering that holds up to twelve blades simultaneously. It works adequately, but the blades closest to the heating elements occasionally come out warped. This is not necessarily a fatal problem because with proper annealing, as described below, the blade can usually be straightened.

Sometimes steel will warp even if heated evenly. This is due to uneven stress already present within the steel prior to heating. Let's say the blade was originally warped when cut out with the cutting torch, or perhaps the original stock had a bend in it. This bend was removed by hammering, or in rolling, which did nothing other than place stresses in the steel to compensate for the warpage. However, during the heating, this stress is removed, and some portion of the original warpage will then become manifest.

Warpage present after quenching is the result of the interplay of the stresses within the steel, in relation to the quality of heat affecting it.

Discoloration

When the steel is at a high temperature, the pores, or areas between the grains of steel, are wide open. Gaseous particles small enough to enter these pores may be absorbed and produce ugly discoloration that can go deeper into the steel. The red-hot blade acts as a sponge for fumes and gasses, so sulfur and other gasses will be absorbed into the surface of the knife if the heat being used is from incomplete, dirty combustion. For example, *hard coal* forge-heating produces ugly yellow blotches of sulfur which deeply stain the steel.

Decarburization

When the blade is heated to an even red, carbon near the surface of the steel can combine with oxygen in the atmosphere and be lost. The longer the blade remains at this temperature, the more carbon will oxidize. Therefore, quench the blade soon after it reaches the crucial temperature. Extensive decarburization produces "carbon runs," resulting in a marble-like texture where the carbon has flowed over the surface of the blade. Of course, as time and temperature increase, so will the amount of carbon loss.

Internal Decay

The molecular structure of steel breaks down when held at a very high temperature. This results in inherently weak steel, and this weakness cannot be completely "erased" by subsequent heat-treatments. The molecular bonds within the steel break up as the grain structure enlarges. Enlarged grain in steel looks "sparkly" where a fresh break is exposed. As to the time and heat required for significant structural damage, I would suspect that an ordinary carbon steel blade heated to a bright orange color for more than five minutes would be weakened. Therefore, heat only to the proper color and quench soon after this color has been obtained evenly over the entire blade. (See heating temperatures, pp. 254–55.)

Hardness, Toughness, and Wear Resistance

What actually gives the steel its wonderful qualities of hardness, toughness, and wear resistance? It is the interaction of the ingredients of the steel with the heat-treating process. But how do the different heat-treatment processes actually affect the steel, and what goes on inside the steel during these treatments that results in these special qualities? Obviously, we must understand this magic process to some degree to have any control over the medium of steel.

The most basic and universal tool steel is a mixture of iron and about 1 percent carbon, with a few other alloys for special properties, plus some impurities. For our purpose here, a basic understanding of the processes for treating carbon steel will suffice. A more thorough treatment of the subject, including alloy steels, is found in the appendix.

Iron, when smeltered from ore, has about 4 percent carbon. This material, when cast into molds, is called *cast iron*. When this material is further refined to a specific analysis and a certain carbon content, then it is some grade of tool steel, and will respond in certain specific ways to various prescribed heat-treatments.

Actually, carbon steel is a combination of iron molecules and molecules of iron carbide. The determining factor for hardness, brittleness, and wear resistance is the state of the iron carbide, hereafter referred to as carbide.

In the softened state, the steel is a mixture of iron and carbide. The carbide is sometimes referred to as cementite. When the steel is heated, the cementite, which makes up only a small percentage of the total mass, begins to melt and dissolve into the surrounding matrix of iron molecules. The point at which this occurs is called the *critical temperature* of that particular steel. The resulting structure of iron with *carbide*, or *cementite*, dissolved, is referred to as *austenite*. The range of temperature within which this austenizing occurs is called the *critical range*.

If the steel cools very quickly, the austenite freezes and forms a hard, needle-like structure called *martensite*. Martensite gives steel its stress, and it is this internal stress which makes the steel hard and brittle.

The factors that produce varying degrees of hardness in the steel are the quenching temperature (the temperature of the steel just prior to the quench), and the speed with which the steel cools. If the steel is heated to the top of its critical range and all the cementite is austenized, and if the steel is then quenched in very cold water, cooling it very rapidly, martensite may form within the steel to such an extent that the steel actually cracks.

Precisely control the quenching temperature and the cooling speed so that just the right amount of stress forms within the steel. Usually an excess of stress is supplied, on purpose. Then, the second treatment, called "tempering" or "drawing," removes this excess stress, leaving the steel sufficiently hard and tough (elastic).

To *temper* the hardened steel, it is heated very carefully to a prescribed temperature. For carbon steel this temperature is somewhere between 400°F. and 600°F., depending upon the desired hardness. As more heat is applied to the steel, more martensite is broken down into *troostite*, also relieving more stress.

The less *internal stress* in a piece of steel, the more external stress it can tolerate before it breaks. It's just like blowing up a balloon—if you supply too much internal stress in the form of air pressure, it doesn't take much external stress to pop it.

So, there you have it—hardness and toughness are, generally speaking, inversely proportional. The harder a piece of steel is tempered, the more brittle it becomes. Proper tempering removes enough of the brittleness without removing too much of the hardness.

The third sought-after quality in a knife blade— wear resistance—is akin to hardness, but not actually the same thing. Two blades of the same hardness may be very different in terms of wear resistance, and it is this latter quality which is the most important quality after toughness in a good blade. The wear resistance of a blade is its ability to hold a good edge—a very important quality.

Wear resistance is controlled primarily by steel chemistry, and not heat-treatment. For low-alloy carbon steel, which is what we are talking about in this chapter, the harder it is, the more wear-resistant it is. However, among different steels at the same hardness level, the higher the carbon content, the higher the wear resistance. Unfortunately, in my experience with different steels, it appears that whenever hardness or wear resistance go up, either because of steel analysis or heat-treatment, toughness goes down. Therefore, as stated earlier, the choice of steel and heat-treatment is a series of trade-offs.

Grain Growth

Another factor in the structural properties of steel is grain growth. Grains of austentite form from ferrite and cementite. As the temperature increases, so does the size of these grains. If steel is heated very far above the critical temperature, the grains become over-large and weaken the steel. Large-grained steel is weaker because there is less surface area between the grains and because the molecular link weakens between them.

For a more complete discussion of the inner drama of steel hardening and chemistry, see the appendix.

Now let's look at the two treatments that make a carbon steel blade hard but not brittle.

Quenching Temperature

The "critical point" is the temperature above which a given type of tool steel must be heated for it to fully harden when quenched. This point varies according to the kind of steel you are using. Before reaching this temperature, steel is dark red and has a shadowy look, but when it has passed through the

Two knives placed in the hot kiln.

"critical transformation," the color is a full, even red glow. For carbon steel, this will probably be 1,425° to 1,550°F. Heating the blade much above 1,550°F. causes increased scale and decarburization and promotes warpage and distortion as well as "grain growth," brittleness, and cracks. Quench the blade, therefore, just as it reaches the full, even red glow of the critical temperature, and not too much hotter.

To best estimate the proper color-temperature of heated steel, the light should be fairly dim so that you can readily observe the glow of the steel. Bright light makes the steel appear much cooler than it actually is. Furthermore, the illumination in the area should be the same each time you harden so that you can be consistent in judging the proper quenching temperature.

There is a simple test that will determine the optimal quenching temperature for a given type of steel and that will insure maximum hardness and durability of the steel. If you use old saw blades, you can test a sample from each blade.

Cut out four or five test strips from the piece of steel you are studying. Put a notch in each piece of steel. One by one, heat each test piece to a slightly different shade of red, from a faint glow to a bright orange yellow. Make a careful note of each color and of the amount of light in the room before quenching each. After you have cooled all of the test pieces, break them, taking note of how easily each one snaps. If a piece bends before breaking, it has not been sufficiently hardened. Be sure they are all as hard as a file.

Observe the *grain growth* within the steel, which you can now see in the broken area of each piece of test steel. Remember, the larger the grain growth, the weaker and more brittle the steel. You can recognize the grain as a rough, sparkly texture. The optimal hardening color is that which hardened well but produced the least observable grain. The best heating temperature should produce an internal grain structure that looks like fine grey velvet.

The Quenching Bath

This treatment should let you quench the steel so that the full potential for hardness is realized, without undue grain growth and internal stresses. The tempering bath may be any liquid that is not too combustible, or air. Different steels are designed and manufactured to be quenched in different types of baths. Oil, brine (salt and water), and forced or still air are coolants most commonly used for quenching. Some steels are designed for *fast* quenching solutions (brine), *medium* quenching speed (a given grade of oil), or *slow* quenching (air). The brine solution cools hot steel faster than oil because it boils briskly at a

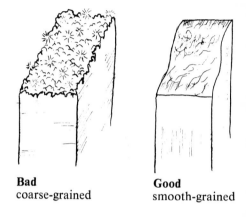

Bad
coarse-grained

Good
smooth-grained

Close-up showing granular structure

lower temperature, and because water conducts heat away faster than oil. The boiling temperature of the mantle (the part of the solution touching the steel) is a determinant of the cooling speed of a quenching bath. Different quenching oils vary in the briskness of the mantle's boil. Air cools the steel even slower than oil because it's less dense and thus has less mass to absorb and carry away the heat. A quenching medium should be chosen recognizing that the faster the steel cools, the more stress will be caused.

Most carbon steel used in making knives hardens quite sufficiently and safely in an oil bath. Since the second step of heat-treatment is drawing out the excess stress, it is not necessary to overstress the steel in a brine bath, but only to produce a moderate excess of hardness in the steel. Assuming you use some common type of high-carbon tool steel, the remaining questions are: what kind of oil, how much, and at what temperature? A very skilled machinist told me that despite what everyone says, any kind of oil will result in about the same tempered hardness. While this would make things easy, I tend to doubt what he says. Oils with different boiling temperatures cool at different speeds.

Thinner oil will move about more briskly when quenching, dissipating the heat faster. Even thick oil, such as old crankcase oil, cools sufficiently fast to harden thin knives. However, very heavy knives, i.e. cleavers and hatchets, often do not harden properly in the thick oil.

If you do not have access to real tempering oil, you can mix equal parts of used crankcase oil with diesel oil. Be sure you are prepared in case of a fire. A good lid for the tempering bath will put any fire out immediately.

In addition to the cooling speed, another factor is the chemical effects different kinds of solutions have on the steel. Remember that at very high temperatures the pores of the steel are wide open to molecular influx. Very knowledgeable people have told me that oil is better than brine because ions or molecules attach themselves within the structure of the steel giving it greater toughness (flexibility) without sacrificing hardness, and that certain types of oil, such as olive oil, or special tempering oils, induce other molecules that further increase the quality of the steel.

From my own observation, olive oil makes a prime quenching bath. The blades cool quickly, and very hard, but seldom crack. They also come out nice and clean and make my shop smell like someone is baking cookies!

Quenching at room temperature, or in slightly warm oil (up to about 140°F.) produces more than enough tension for a hard blade, causing neither breakage nor even small checks. The bath should be deep enough to comfortably immerse the longest knives to a depth of at least 6 inches.

When quenching, have the blade lengthwise above the bath surface, and plunge the blade into the oil as quickly as possible, moving the blade gently up and down within the solution for several seconds. Do not remove the blade until it has stopped vibrating from shock (usually about five to fifteen seconds). The bath will, of course, get warm if you temper many knives successively, so make sure it is large enough (say five gallons) if you plan to do any large-scale tempering. I use a five-gallon oil bath. If the oil becomes 140°F. or so, or the slightest bit hot to the touch, it may be too warm to harden effectively, and you should wait until it cools.

After the knife is quenched, test the hardness with a file. The file should not be able to bite the knife blade. If it does bite the steel, then the knife is not properly hardened. Either it was not heated sufficiently, or the oil bath was too warm, or else the blade is not made from high-carbon steel.

Hold blade parallel
to bath surface
prior to quenching

Oil bath
suspended
in water

Tempering the Blade

The second heat-treatment softens the steel slightly, to a precise hardness—the point where the brittleness is removed, and yet the blade is still sufficiently hard. There is a theoretical optimum—the point of maximum toughness—that any piece of steel can reach, depending on its metallurgical characteristics and its shape. This is the point where, when sufficient stress is applied, the steel will just begin to bend as it breaks. There is a distinction between bending and flexing. When something flexes, it will snap back to its original position. When the thing bends, however, it will not snap all the way back. A blade softer than optimum toughness will bend too easily, but will seldom break or snap, while a blade harder than optimum will tend to break too easily.

There are factors to consider in tempering other than optimum toughness, such as "sharpen-ability" and the kind of usage the knife is designed for. For example, a vegetable knife should, in my opinion, be tempered softer than a survival knife. This is because the long vegetable blade is a lot of work to sharpen while subject to much less strenuous usage. But, again, this is up to the discretion of the individual knifemaker.

Tempering Colors

Controlling hardness, or inner stress, is referred to as "tempering." Clean the *hardened* blade to an even shine with an old 80- or 120-grit belt, then heat the entire blade slowly and evenly in an oven to about 450°F. until it turns from grey silver steel to the desired color, and then cool it. Referring to the color chart, you will see that the steel, when heated, turns from a silver grey to a light gold tint and then to darker and darker shades of bronze, becoming reddish, then a bright and very striking vermillion, and into a light blue or peacock, and finally into the dark blue of soft steel. Steel becomes progressively softer through this color range, with the cutoff point between hardened and softened steel being between the peacock blue and dark blue.

I have found the point of best compromise for most carbon saw-blade steel knives somewhere in the medium straw range. I usually temper at the medium straw range, because the blade seems still hard enough but is nearly impossible to break. If I want a particularly hard blade, I will temper at the light straw color. Some makers of vegetable knives draw the steel to a softer state, say to a vermillion.

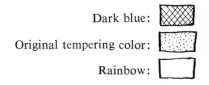

Dark blue:
Original tempering color:
Rainbow:

Annealing the Backbone and Handle Areas

The third part of the heat-treating process consists of carefully heating and thus softening the handle area and the back and center of the blade just down to the ground edge. Turn these areas to a deep blue, but the colors must not run into the cutting edge or the hardness of the edge will be lost and the knife will have to be rehardened. I use a small welding tip for this, and have a bucket of water handy so I can dip the ground area of the blade should the heat begin to run too close to the edge. If you douse the entire blade, it may regain its hardness while remaining blue; then when you go to straighten the blade, it may crack.

Use a pair of Vise Grips, clamping the tang and heating the blade along the back edge about a ½ inch from the tip, or, if there is a sharpened top edge, just behind the last sharpened area. If you heat on one side more than another, the blade will warp away from the flame. Aim the flame slightly away from the edge to prevent the heat from running down to the edge too quickly. With a wide blade I run the flame across the flat area, first on one side, then on the

Cooling the ground edge

other, to avoid warping. Work along the complete length of the blade in full, even strokes until it begins to streak blue, then continue carefully until the blue has run down just to the lower part of thick metal above the edge. Stop the application of the heat a little before the blue runs to the top of the ground area so the blade can cool just a little before you dip the cutting edge in water. Allow the blade to cool for about twenty seconds and carefully douse the edge to avoid further heat-travel toward the edge. Then, grip the back of the blade with Vise Grips and heat the tang of the knife. Be sure the handle is a nice, even blue, merging with the blue area on the blade. If the handle is not turned to an even blue, you may have trouble when you attempt to drill the rivets. Do not overheat an area that will easily reharden due to air cooling, because this will cause considerable trouble when drilling the handle or straightening the blade.

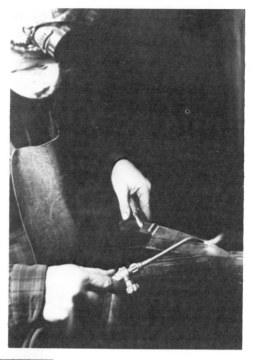

Carefully heating the unground parts of a chef's blade.

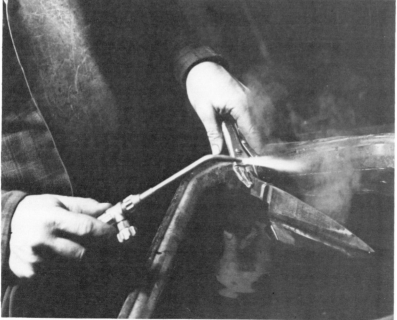

Dipping the edge of the heated blade in water so it will retain its hardness in the face of the advancing heat.

Heat the handle area with the torch so that it will be soft enough to straighten and drill. Heat the steel underneath the bolster area sufficiently, or it may crack at the bolster if you have to straighten it there, or possibly even during use.

Annealing Underneath the Bolster

If you are annealing a knife with a brazed-on bolster (see chapter 12), heat the brass on the top and on both sides until the steel on each side of the brass begins to turn blue. This anneals the steel underneath the brass.

Look at the entire blade. It should be deep blue, except for the area from the cutting edge to about ¼ or ¾ inch up. Only the area that will eventually be sharpened should be light straw to a vermillion color, depending upon how hard the blade was tempered.

Spark Test for Hardness

A good way to double-check the hardness of a blade, and especially to see if it is hardened evenly all along the whole edge, is to observe the sparks that fly

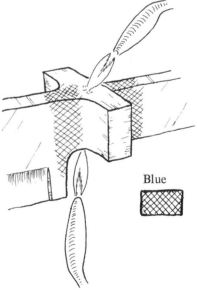

Blue

Annealing the brazed-on bolster

when you run the edge across the belt grinder. The sparks should be bright and complex. If they are dim or nonexistent, double-check the hardness in that area. Bright, complex bursts in the spark stream indicate hardened carbon steel.

How Hard Is Hard?

While the subject of hardness is covered in more detail in the appendix, let's look at some of the basics here so we have a better idea of what we are doing. Hardness is the resistance to indentation. Within any one type of steel, hardness is almost directly proportional to wear resistance—the harder it is, the more wear-resistant it is. Remember, too, the harder it is, the more brittle it is. There are exceptions, especially among the higher alloy steels.

A hardness tester is one of the basic tools of metallurgists, when it comes to tool steels. There are several types, but the one most commonly used to test knives is called a Rockwell hardness tester. It measures the resistance to indentation of a piece of steel and rates the sample on a scale called the Rockwell C-scale, which runs from twenty through sixty-eight. The higher the number, the harder the sample. Generally, a knife edge should be somewhere between fifty-seven to fifty-eight and sixty-three or sixty-four. Values very far below or above this range are either too soft or too hard to make a good blade.

Saw-blade steel should be tempered to a hardness of between sixty and sixty-two. This is achieved by tempering temperatures 350°F. to 450°F., as shown on the tempering chart for L6, p. 258. Tempering within this heat range should give you tempering colors between a light silvery straw and a medium straw.

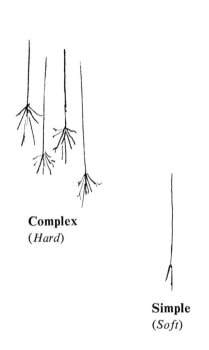

Complex
(*Hard*)

Simple
(*Soft*)

Chapter 8

Trueing Up the Blade

Straightening the blade can be a problem. You have successfully ground, hardened, tempered, and softened the blade in the appropriate places. Possibly you have brazed or soldered additional metal pieces to the shank. Due to uneven heating or cooling in these treatments, the blade may be warped or bent or twisted. In fact, it may be ruined.

If the knife is heated mostly on one side (for example, near the kiln heating element), it will flex away from the heat, bending the blade. As it cools, it will "freeze" in this position.

Place the blade on a perfectly flat surface and carefully observe its straightness. It may have one or more curves in it, and may even be slightly twisted like a corkscrew. Since there are no further radical operations to be performed that will warp the blade, except possibly etching, this is the time to make it as straight as possible. Straighten the blade before removing the tempering colors so that you know exactly where the softened and hardened areas are.

Only hammer in the dark blue area, because it may crack or shatter if you strike it in a hardened area.

Hammering the Blade

Place a heavy piece of scrap leather between the anvil and blade to reduce the shock to your hands and ears, as well as to the blade. You can straighten a blade more easily without cracking the edge with such a cushion. Using a smooth, heavy, rounded hammer, simply beat the blade flat. Place the concave side down on the padded or slightly concave anvil. Strike with the center of the hammer head, not the edge, or you will dent sweet little smiles all over the side of the blade.

Hit it easily at first, then harder. You can feel the vibration that the blade gives off when struck, and you can hear its sound. If it feels hard and unyielding and sounds high-pitched, it might not be properly annealed in the spot you are striking. Look carefully at that spot and see if it really is a full, even blue color. If it is a lighter grey color in spots, go back and anneal more fully and carefully to an even, deep blue so you can adequately straighten the blade.

Beat along the center of the blade until it seems pretty flat. Then, look along the edge and along the back and proceed until the blade lies flat on a smooth table top.

Untwisting the Blade

A twisted blade is a more difficult problem. In this case you look down the edge and then down the back, and see curves in different directions. This can be very difficult to fix with a hammer and anvil, but if the blade is not too thick, you can simply untwist it with a wrench and vise.

If it is thicker steel, too stiff to bend on your vise, heat along the back from the convex side of that curve. You can get a little of the twist out that way; then try beating out the rest. When hammering, strike along the convex side of the back of the knife, trying to make it about as concave as the blade. Then, turn the knife over and hammer along the blue just above the cutting edge, until the edge is straight. Check the overall knife. If it still has a twist in it, repeat, this time exaggerating the first hammering step.

Heat from one side

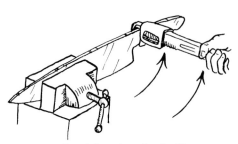

Straightening the knife

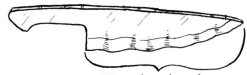

Warped cutting edge

Wavy Edge

Another distressing form of warpage is when the cutting edge is wavy, while the body of the blade is relatively straight. This usually is due to a too-thin grinding job, which causes uneven cooling in the oil bath. The edge, which is very thin, cools first, and, as it tries to shrink, it is prevented from doing so by the still expanded shank. Thus the steel along the edge stretches a little. Then, a second or so later the shank contracts, pulling the thin edge with it and causing it to buckle like a ribbon. Place the blade on an unpadded anvil and hammer along, and just above, the cutting edge, just inside the blue all along the wavy area on both sides of the blade.

Because hammer blows flatten and thus "stretch" the steel, what you are doing is lengthening the shank of the blade to restretch the thin ribbon of steel along the cutting edge.

Consider tempering the edge a little softer, say to a light vermillion, to reduce the possibility of cracking the edge during the straightening operation.

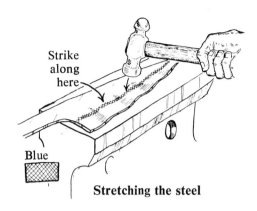

Stretching the steel

Straightening at the Bolster

A knife with a brazed bolster or finger guard that has warped or bent at the bolster presents a special straightening problem.

The bolster prevents the blade from lying flat across the anvil. Carefully heat the knife at the bent spot on the convex side only; this should improve the line somewhat.

If the blade is still not perfectly in line after heating one side of the bolster, put the blade in a heavy vise, right up to the bolster, and use a heavy crescent wrench as a lever. However, before doing this, double-check the anneal under the bolster by heating it carefully on one side.

Prevention is the solution in such a case—be *very*

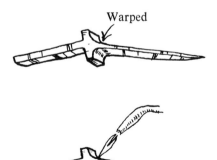

careful tempering bolstered knives. Heat them evenly and you probably will not have this problem.

If you plan to *silver-solder* or *pin* any additional pieces to the blade or handle, such as a brass bolster, turn to chapter 6 and complete that operation, then return to the section on drilling the rivet or pin holes. It is preferable to solder the bolster before drilling the holes because you can do a better job of placing the holes once you can see and feel the knife with the bolster on.

Chapter 9

Regrinding and Polishing the Blade

If the knife is intended to have a fine (thin) edge, you should do the last portion of the grinding after tempering, because a very thin edge will warp during the heating process. However, grinding the edge after it is tempered is also risky, since grinding heat can remove some of the hardness. You must go slow if you do not have a water-cooled belt grinder, dipping the

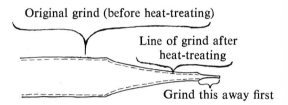

Typical blade cross section showing stock removal before and after tempering

Before starting to regrind, use a micrometer to double-check the thickness and evenness of the blade.

blade in water after every one or two passes across the wheel. Use a new belt for this process because new abrasives grind with less heat than grindstones. I use 40-grit for this step.

Removing the Grinder Marks

To prepare the blade for polishing, you will need to regrind the blade with an 80-grit belt, if you have not already done so. Then repeat this process with 120-, 240-, 320-, 480-, and 600-grit belts.

You do not have to select these particular grit sizes, but the idea is to start with a belt coarse enough to remove the obvious grinder marks and other gross blemishes. Follow with a treatment just coarse enough to remove these marks, and so on, stepping down the size of the grinding marks to around 600. The 600-grit marks can be buffed away, leaving a mir-

Various ways of holding the blade against the sanding wheel. Moisture is used to keep the blade cool during grinding. If you do not have a water-cooled set-up, use bare hands to hold the hardened blade. The sensitivity of your bare hands to the blade will help prevent overheating it.

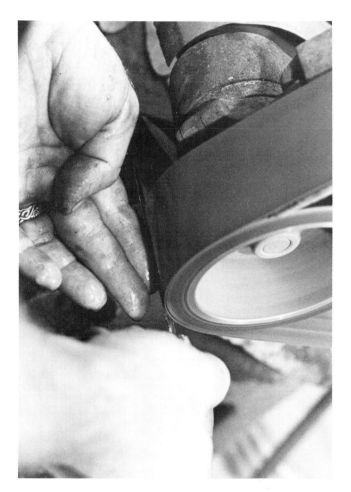

ror finish. This is important, not only for the appearance of the blade, but for ease of cleaning.

Keep two things in mind each time you go over the blade. First, do not heat the cutting edge. If it turns blue, or significantly darkens, you either have to carefully grind that part of the blade off, or retemper the blade. Second, maintain and perfect the clean and well-defined grinding lines of the knife. Occasionally vary the angle of grinding slightly so you can see if you are getting down past previous grit marks.

Regrinding the blade using a work rest to steady the work. This is essential, for me, at least, to achieve a good straight grinding line.

If you are regrinding a blade more than 2½ inches long, you can achieve a straighter, more precise grinding line by using a work rest on the belt grinder. This is a U-shaped bracket like the one described in the bench-grinder section of the Tools chapter. However, this one doesn't have to be quite as adjustable. The work wheel on a belt grinder, unlike a grindstone, does not change size constantly, although it should be easy to move out of the way when you change belts.

Whenever grinding a tempered blade, use only a very sharp grinding implement, like a sharp stone or a brand new abrasive cloth, because the sharper it is, the less heat is generated within the steel.

A 120-grit belt will remove all the 80-grit grinding marks and put the final touches on the blade, such as tapering the cutting edge to your liking, working over the tip, and perhaps making the hollow grind deeper, clearer, and more precise.

A view from the operator's position, looking down at a medium chef's knife being buffed.

Repeat this operation using a new 240-grit belt, and so on up to a 600-grit. Finer grit steps are really more like polishing operations than grinding steps, so I change the wheel on my belt grinder to one that is made from softer rubber, with a slightly rounded face and corners. This allows me to easily remove any cuts that may have been caused by the corner of the wheel on the previous step, and keep myself from making any new ones.

Leave the upper edge of the blade rough and finish it when you polish the handle. This keeps the top of the handle and the back of the blade flush and smooth flowing.

After the 600-grit polishing step, buff the blade, and then carefully wrap the polished area of the blade in masking tape. This protects the finish from scratches and rust while the knife is being completed. The blade will be buffed again after the handle is completed.

If you want to etch designs into the blade, do so after the drilling operation, before putting the handle on. Buff the blade before it is etched. Skip to the chapter on etched designs, then after the etching is completed, start the chapter on handle construction. The entire knife, both blade and handle, is buffed in one operation.

A Short Cut

If you do not wish to repeat finer and finer belt-grinding steps, perhaps because you do not have all the grit sizes, you can polish after, say, the 240-grit or 320-grit step. This produces a nice shine to the steel, but not a mirror polish. Prior to buffing, go over the blade once again with the belt machine, this time using an old, dull 320-grit belt with buffing compound rubbed into it. This does not produce a shine, but it's terrific for removing scratches and preparing the steel to take a handsome finish when buffed. Rub stick abrasive against the belt when it is in motion, just as you would on the buffing wheel.

Chapter 10

Drilling Rivet Holes

If the knife has a slab handle, you will most likely fasten the slabs to the shank with epoxy cement and rivets or pins. In addition to the holes for the rivets or pins, other holes will be drilled in the shank to be filled with epoxy. These holes form internal "epoxy rivets" which strengthen the bond of the slabs to the shank.

Placement of the Holes

Carefully determine the location of the rivet or pin holes. If you use pins, there is more freedom of placement because they are smaller and can be beveled if they are in a curved area of the handle. Rivet heads should be put in large flat areas of the handle or the edge of the rivet heat may be ground away. (See drawing, p. 172.)

After placing the rivet or pin holes, determine the placement for a minimum of six or eight epoxy rivet holes. There should be at least two epoxy rivets on each side of each metal pin or rivet hole. Place epoxy rivet holes in any broad areas on the handle. The more of these you have, the more invincible the bond between the tang and slabs.

Changing the Placement of a Metal Rivet Hole

If you drill a hole in the wrong place, say $1/16$ inch off center, you can move the hole slightly by filing it in the direction you want with a round chain saw file of the proper size.

If you start a hole in the wrong place, let's say too far to one side of the handle, and it's not too deep, you

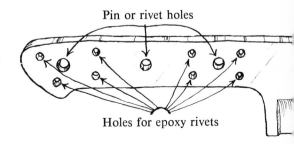

Pin or rivet holes

Holes for epoxy rivets

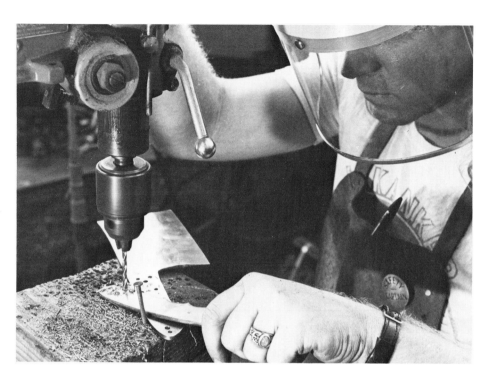

Moving a hole that was started a little off center.

can move the hole slightly by tilting the workpiece. Do this by simply placing something under the side of the handle you want the hole to move away from. The tip of the drill will "skate" across the steel in the downhill direction. Be careful not to break the bit.

Losing Weight

You can reduce the total weight of the knife by drilling extra epoxy rivet holes in the tang. This also tips the center of balance more toward the blade, if this is what you want. You are almost ready to begin drilling all these holes.

Drill Bits

You should be able to use ordinary high-speed drill bits if the handle area has been perfectly annealed. Use a cobalt drill bit, which is a little harder (and more expensive), in case you hit hard spots. You

will probably have to order them from a tool and dye supply house.

For the inexpensive metal rivets, use a bit size that is only slightly larger (say $1/64$ inch) than the rivet shaft. (See chapter 11.) For the ordinary $3/16$-inch brake-shoe rivets use a $13/64$-inch drill. The oversized rivet holes allow space for the rivets to expand slightly when hammered together. If you're using pins instead of rivets, choose a drill exactly the same size as the pin because it does not need room to expand. It does not matter what size the epoxy rivet holes are.

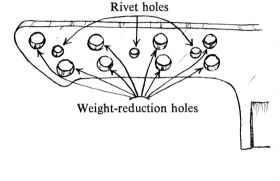

Rivet holes

Weight-reduction holes

Sharpening a Drill Bit

The drill bit becomes dull after a certain amount of use. Sharpen it at once. If you go on using it, the bit will heat up and lose its temper, or it will shatter. Once you get the knack of it, it takes only a few seconds to sharpen a drill bit.

Take a good look at a new or properly sharpened bit. Observe the cutting edges and how they angle into the stock as the drill spins.

See how nice and neat the facets are that form the cutting edge. They are square, not rounded. If they curve, they slope backward so the highest point along

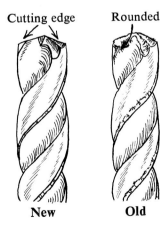

Cutting edge   Rounded

New   **Old**

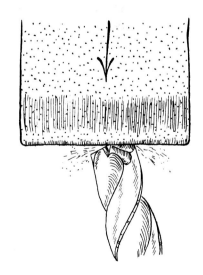

the tip is the cutting edge itself. Otherwise, the drill would "skate" on the surface of the stock. The cutting edge must be properly angled into the stock as the drill turns. Observe the new bit closely. Then, look at the bit that does not perform well. Are the cutting edges rounded? Is the facet cut at the proper angle?

Using a new 240-grit belt, carefully grind the edges sharp. Hold the facet up to the wheel and, with the cutting edge toward you (up), twist the bit slowly as you grind down the facet.

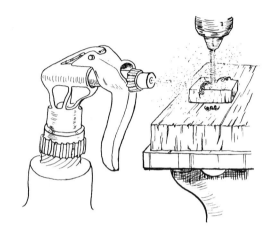

Remember, a dull edge produces a visible glint. So, grind the facet down until the glint along the cutting edge disappears. Dip the drill in water so you do not overheat it.

Grind each facet the same amount to keep the drill symmetrical. The cutting edge should be slightly higher than the rest of the facet. Be careful not to round off the tip where the two facets come together, but keep them sharp. You can cut away the back of the facet somewhat to make the bit sharper at the tip.

Use Tooling Fluid

Ordinary water is an adequate and nonmessy tooling fluid to use when drilling the handles. I use a good-quality plastic atomizing spray bottle. If you use an oil-base tooling fluid, remember to remove all traces of oil before attempting to glue on the handle.

Chapter 11

Rivets and Pins, Pins and Rivets

The scales are held onto the tang with epoxy glue and brass rivets or pins. The rivets have a head on each end that mechanically hold the scales tightly against the shank. The pins simply form a metal connection between the two slabs, being held in place by the epoxy glue.

Brass Pins

Pins are the simplest means of holding the scales on. They are made from short lengths of brazing rod. The surface of the rod is scored with concentric rings on a fresh, coarse abrasive belt. This is done by holding the rod against the unsupported belt at a right angle to it, and turning the rod. The deeply grooved surface aids them in being locked tightly in place by the epoxy.

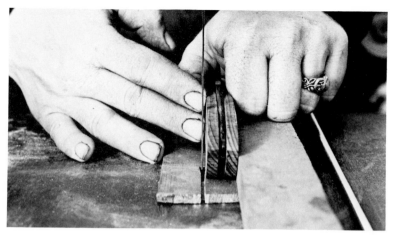

This sequence shows how to cut
all of the pins an equal and
proper length. A piece of wood
is clamped the proper distance
from the blade. This forms a
stop, or jig, to hold the pinstock
at the right length. The piece of
brass that the pinstock is riding on
gives a little clearance so the
fingers can grip it.

Cut the rods into lengths only slightly longer than the width of the scale handle. Bevel off the corners of the pins at one end so they slide through the hole easily. I will tell you how to set them in the section on gluing the handle with pins in chapter 13.

Inexpensive Rivets

Ordinary brake-shoe rivets are excellent for holding the handle slabs together. You can get them in either steel or brass from any good auto-supply store. The ones you are interested in come in two size ranges: the five series and the seven series. The rivets have a long shank with a flat head. At the end of the shank is a hole about $3/16$-inch deep.

"Seven" series (*Female*)   **"Five" series** (*Male*)   **"Driven into marriage"**

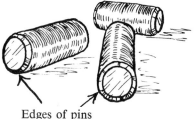

Edges of pins beveled off

Although they were not intended to be used in this manner, it turns out that the shank of the size five rivets can be hammered into the hole at the end of the size seven rivets, forming a very tight male-female press fit.

Improving the Rivets

The tightness of the fit can be increased by grinding off the tips of the five series (male) rivets down past the hole. The portion pounded into the female rivet will then be solid, rather than tubular. The tubular tip of the male rivet could collapse slightly, possibly slipping out at some future time.

Order size five (male) rivets about three sizes longer than you actually need, and grind them off past the hole. Grind a variety of lengths and put each size in a separate container. Bevel them off so they will "find" the female rivet easily.

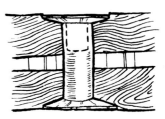

Slight bevel

Before final grinding

After final grinding

You want rivets no shorter than $3/16$ inch nor longer than $5/16$ inch. A variety of sizes within this range provides flexibility in matching with the different sizes of female rivets for a particular handle thickness. The female rivet should be the longer of the two, reaching most of the way through the rivet hole. You should have a full range of lengths for seven-series rivets.

Cut-away view

Making a Countersink Bit

Countersink the rivet head flush with the outside of the slab. You need a drill bit which is precisely the size and shape of the rivet head and shaft for this.

Functionally, the bit consists of a long pilot shaft that fits snugly into the rivet hole, and two blades that cut away the material, forming the countersink hole. Countersinking bits are available in many sizes, but you can construct a countersink bit from an existing

A countersink bit with a matching drill bit. This one was made from an old screwdriver.

flat wood-drill bit or the tip of a flat screwdriver. Reshape the bit or screwdriver tip to a $^{13}/_{64}$-inch-diameter pilot shaft about ¼ inch long, and cut the edges exactly symmetrical, the width of the rivet head and at the same angle. Do this simple machining task on the belt grinder, or use a thin cutoff wheel on a small grinding arbor.

The angle of the blades that cut the countersink hole must be the same as the angle of the underside of the rivet head so there is no air space between the rivet head and the scale. The countersink bit is, of course, used with the drill press.

The outside of the rivet head should be sunk just below the surface of the scale.

How to Set the Brake-shoe Rivets

To set the rivet, insert the size seven (female)

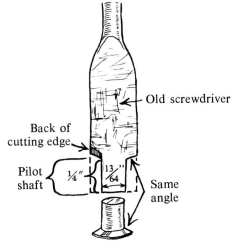

Rivet is same width and length as pilot shaft

rivet and then turn over the handle and lay in the modified size five (male) rivet. Use a long size seven, going nearly through to the countersink area on the other side. Select a female that sticks above the end of the size five rivet by no more than $3/16$ inch. Tap around with your hammer until you find the hole. A pair of needle-nosed pliers will help get the rivet started. Or, push the size five rivet all the way in, so the head is sealed in the countersink hole, turn over the handle, drop in the size seven rivet, and tap lightly until you feel it go in.

Prior to setting, the rivet should stick up no more than $3/16$ inch or it will be too long when set and you will be tempted to compress it with the hammer, making it thicker and possibly splitting the wood. I have seen handles begin to split up to six months later from the pressure caused by the compressed rivet being too thick.

The idea is to have the rivets fit as snugly as possible, but not overly tight.

Removing a Rivet

If one of the rivets was improperly set, or if the head becomes damaged during the handle-shaping process, you must replace it with a new one. The

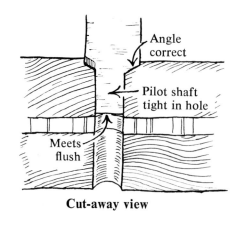

Cut-away view

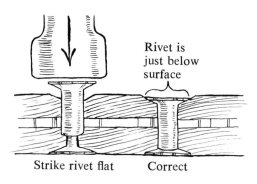

Cut-away view

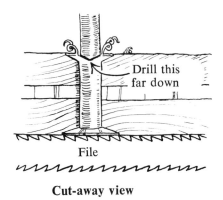

Cut-away view

easiest way I know to remove the rivet is to drill out the rivet head with a $^{13}/_{64}$-inch drill bit and then knock the shaft of the rivet through with a punch. If the rivet gets hot while it is being drilled, breaking the epoxy bond, you may have trouble keeping the rivet from spinning. Prevent this by placing a file underneath the rivet. The rivet head will catch in the teeth of the file. After the rivet is removed, you may have to ream out the countersink hole a little in preparation for the new rivet.

Knifemaker's Rivets

There are rivets made expressly for knife handles. They are the screw-on type, with long heads. After countersinking the heads, the portion remaining is beveled off with the belt grinder. These rivets are available at knifemaker's supply houses. They run about twenty-five times more expensive than the brake-shoe type.

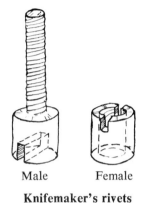

Male   Female

Knifemaker's rivets

Cut away view

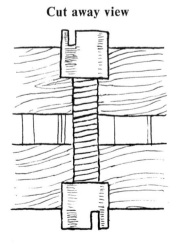

Grind away flat

Chapter 12

Handle Materials

You probably have your own ideas of the handle materials you like best. Here are a few of my thoughts on the subject. Factors to consider are beauty, durability, weight, warmth to the touch, and economy. Stability is also a prime factor in handle material choice—whether there is a tendency to shrink in dry weather and to expand in wet weather, and whether or not there is a tendency to *check*, i.e., to form cracks easily. Usually, but not always, the denser and less porous a material is, the more stable it is.

Wood

If you treasure the beauty and warmth of wood as I do, you will find the darker, harder woods of the tropics to be premium. Lighter colored woods are usually not as hard, and tend to look dirty and washed out in time, while many of the very hard, darker, and densely grained resinous woods become more beautiful with age. I would especially recommend such tropical hardwoods as lignum vitae cocobolo, pau-Brazil, partridge wood, ebony, greenheart, rosewood, and padauk. Of the domestic woods, I have used manzanita burl, black walnut burl, applewood, desert ironwood, birdseye maple, and others. You may find some other excellent types. Use only wood that is close grained, hard, and beautiful.

Milling the Wood

Using the band saw, I cut all my wood into strips about an inch to 2 or 3 inches wide, and from ⅝ inch

Uncut log

to 1 inch thick, and about 2½ feet long. They fit nicely in my drying rack, and I can select different size pieces for different knives. I cut the handles right out of the strips of wood with the band saw. Be sure that the pieces are cut smooth and straight, and are of even thickness.

There are two types of wood in each tree: the sapwood, which grows on the outside near the bark, and the heartwood, which grows in the center of the tree. Usually the sapwood is much lighter in color and more porous. The heartwood is the most suitable for handle construction.

Always make the cuts so that the most beautiful grain patterns become visible. The side of the handle should be parallel with the side grain of the structure.

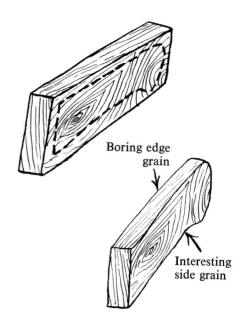

Boring edge grain

Interesting side grain

Handles from Animals

Stag handles, though undeniably beautiful, present some formidable problems. Most of the available stag is from North America, and native stag shrinks and swells with weather conditions, warps, and in time becomes porous. European stag, on the other hand, is superior in this regard. The best kind of stag for knife handles, I am told, comes from India. Both the European and Indian staghorn are becoming scarce. Personally, I do not like the idea of taking a beautiful and rare deer just to make a knife handle. I am not adamant about this; I simply haven't gone out of my way to get rare stag for handles. I feel the same way about ivory, and whale's teeth of course. It would be nice to take the pressure off these poor creatures. However, I do use such materials if they come my way.

Some ivory, bone, and stag antler is taken with no harm to the animal. Whale's teeth are gathered from the ocean floor in certain areas, and tusk ivory is gathered from such sources as Siberia (mammoth tusk) and African elephants' breeding and "burial" grounds. Certain types of stag are gathered after the antlers are shed in the fall, before they begin to decompose. Water buffalo horn also makes good knife handles.

Bone "stag" handles are made from beef bone, particularly the shin bone. This is bleached and carved to look rough, like stag. However, beef bone tends to be very thin, and is suitable only for very small knives or folding knives, or for the top layer of a composite handle.

Micarta

Some very beautiful handles are made from plastic products such as Micarta. This is phenolic resin impregnated into some semiporous material such as wood, paper, linen cloth, or cotton. It comes in a wide range of colors and textures, and some types rival the finest woods and ivory for visual beauty. The advantage of Micarta and other plastics is that they don't shrink and expand with changes in humidity, and they are very resistant to splitting and cracking.

Most of the woods, animal material, and many types of Micarta are available in certain knifemaker's supply houses.

Moisture and Stability

If you select an organic material, such as wood, bone, or ivory, the moisture content of the material must be taken into account.

This factor is particularly important because wood or bone shrinks as it dries. Damp wood on a knife can shrink below the level of the tang, and away from the rivets and bolster, and actually become loose. This is most upsetting to someone who has paid a fair price for a handmade knife.

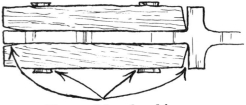

The wood has shrunk!
(*Slightly exaggerated*)

The degree of dryness is crucial to properly attaching the handle because any piece of wood or bone reacts to humidity by contracting and expanding. Wood must be sufficiently dry to start with so that the change is minimal. Expansion of the wood in wet climates is almost unnoticeable, but a little contraction breaks apart the cement, leaving gaps that weaken the handle and collect moisture and crud and look terrible. So I repeat, start out with wood that is plenty dry (but not parched).

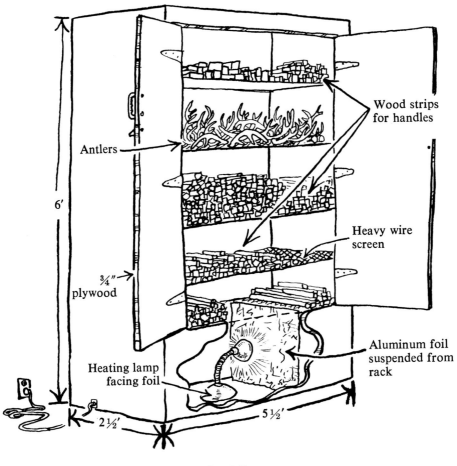

Drying kiln
(*Cut-away view*)

A Drying Kiln

I made a drying kiln out of plywood, with 1 inch by 1 inch fir frame. It is 6 feet high by 5 feet wide and 2½ feet deep. The shelves are heavy wire mesh that allows the warm air to move around freely. The doors open all the way to give easy access to the shelves. It is "powered" by a 350-watt electric heater aimed at a tinfoil reflector which diffuses the heat.

A drying kiln is indispensable for me because I live near the coast, where it is always damp. It is probably indispensable to any knifemaker who does not live in the desert.

Chapter 13

Making a Full-tang Scale Handle

We have covered nearly everything you need to know to build a full-tang scale handle. You have a blade and tang ready. Perhaps there is a bolster and maybe a butt plate. The handle material is ready and dry.

If you are fitting scales to a bolster, skip ahead and read that section on page 160 first, then come back and read from here.

Cutting Out the Slabs

Trace the handle on a piece of handle stock. Start with a piece that, when added to the thickness of the tang, is just a little wider than the desired handle. Cut out the shape on the band saw, then cut it into two equal halves. The two pieces are exactly the same shape. Cut out the handle very carefully, just a hair longer than the outside line of the tang. The more precisely you cut the handle, the less work you will have beveling the slabs flush with the tang. Watch for cracks and checks in the wood.

Fitting the Scales to the Tang

First, using a new 80-grit belt, make the inside surface of the scales perfectly flat by pressing against the flat belt support on the sander. I usually flip the scales inside out first, because the planed surface of the stock's outside is flatter and smoother than the

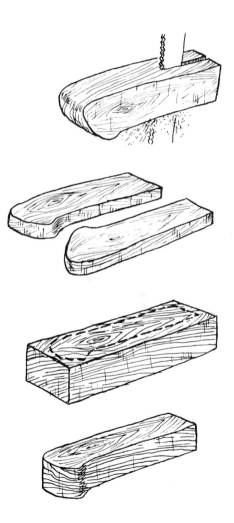

band-sawed split inside, producing a perfectly smooth, flat surface to join to the tang.

Be sure that the belt is crossing the belt support smoothly. I had to weld a thin piece of steel on top of my machine's support to make it high enough to stretch the belt smoothly across its face. When you push the slab against the sander, hold it with two hands, one at each end of the slab. If you use one hand, press very lightly. This insures even, steady pressure against the belt. It is very easy to ruin a scale by bowing it from too much pressure in the middle. Check the flatness by putting both slabs together and holding them up to the light.

Carefully clean the tang with the belt grinder. If there is a bolster, be sure to clean right up to the brass. Now, place the scales onto the tang and hold the handle up to the light to see if there are any spaces. The tang may have slight waves you had not

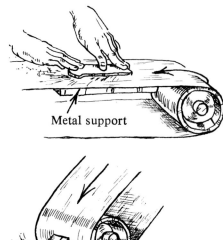

Metal support

Separate pieces
held together

This knifemaker uses only one hand to flatten the slab, but he has had a lot of practice.

noticed until now. Hammer them out. Or there may be a slight, almost imperceptible twist in the tang which prevents the scales from seating correctly. Remove it by untwisting with a vise and wrench.

It is essential to the function and the appearance of the finished knife that there be no gaps between the scale and tang. Epoxy will completely fill any gap, but it will be unsightly and possibly weaker. This is one of the features people study when considering the purchase of a knife.

Unless you are fitting the scales against a metal bolster or finger guard, bevel the end of the slabs nearest the blade. This area will be very difficult to work once it is against the shank, so finish this area now.

Checking for cracks between the handle and tang.

Straightening a tang on a railroad-track anvil. We use a special one-clawed hammer for this operation.

Put the two together and hold them tightly as one unit and bevel them very carefully against the wheel of the sander. Start with about an 80-grit belt, then the 120-grit and finish with about a 240-grit belt. Turn the scales over and fair down the outsides to just slightly thicker than you will want them in the finished knife. Hold them evenly as you did when you flattened the insides.

Beveling and polishing the front ends of the slabs.

Fitting the Scales to the Bolster

Trim the inside of the bolster area with a file so it's neat and clean and perfectly square to receive the slabs.

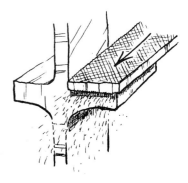

Fitting the scales to a knife with a bolster is, of course, a little tricky. Hopefully you cut the pieces slightly oversize. Carefully grind down the end of

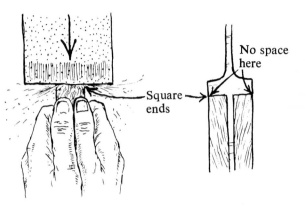

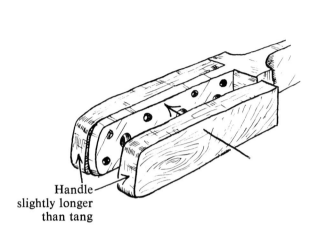

Handle
slightly longer
than tang

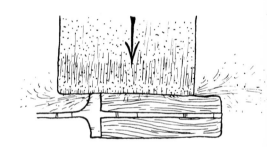

Leveling off the bolster

each scale with an 80-grit belt until it precisely fits against the bolster. Use a file to get them exact. If you have made the scales a little too long to start with, you have room for error and can trim a little off here and there until it fits exactly. Hold it up to the light and see if there are any gaps between scale and bolster. Grind off the tips of the bolster so they are flush with the handle material.

If the scale must fit between a bolster and a butt, the job is more difficult because there is no room for mistakes. You have to get it on the first try, or you will quickly find that the scale has become too short, and you have to start over again with another piece.

The butt-plate handle is more difficult and should not be attempted until you have mastered the bolster-only model.

Drilling the Holes in the Slabs

After you have gotten the scales to fit perfectly onto the tang, you are ready to drill the holes for the metal rivets or pins. Clamp one slab onto the tang

Butt plate

No gaps!

with a pair of Vise Grips, and with the slab side down, drill the holes in the slab using the predrilled rivet holes in the tang as a template. Make sure the scales are snug against the bolster and that the holes are perfectly lined up. After removing the first slab, clamp the second one against the other side of the tang and drill it in the same fashion.

Now drill shallow holes in the inside of the slab adjacent to each of the epoxy rivet holes. I do this by marking the handle material with a pencil, and then removing the clamped-on tang so I can see exactly how deep to go. Obviously, it would be a disaster if you went too deep and the hole emerged on the other side of the slab. I drill them about ⅛-inch deep.

If you will be setting the slabs with rivets instead of pins, drill out the countersink holes for the rivet heads, as pictured on pages 147–48.

1. Drilling through the pre-drilled tang to make a pin hole in the slab. The slab and the tang are clamped together with a pair of Vise Grips. The block of wood supporting the slab has a U-shaped section removed to make room for the Vise Grips. This way all the holes are always drilled at the same angle. Otherwise the pins can be impossible to get through the holes.

2. Marking the spots where the shallow epoxy rivet holes will be drilled in the inside of the slab.

Clamping the Scales to the Shank

Before mixing up the epoxy, wait! Get your clamps ready. You will need three or four C clamps.

If your knife has a bolster, you should modify a fairly large clamp so that it can hold the scales up against the bolster as shown. Use a cutoff wheel to grind the slot in the end of the C clamp. Lacking that, use a hacksaw. The two or three other clamps will push the sides of the scales in.

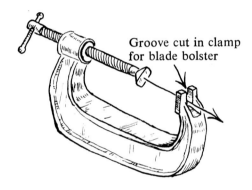

Groove cut in clamp for blade bolster

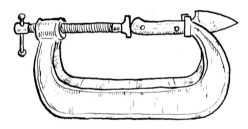

Knife in place

Clamp the whole thing together once for practice before mixing the epoxy! Remember, you do not need the modified clamp going lengthwise unless you have a bolster or finger guard on the knife.

Go back to chapter 11 and prepare the rivets or pins. Make sure the brass rivets or pins are the correct length. Practice setting them so that you can do it smoothly after the epoxy is mixed.

Epoxy Glue

This is a very strong plastic adhesive-filler that is activated and becomes hard after its two constituent parts are mixed together.

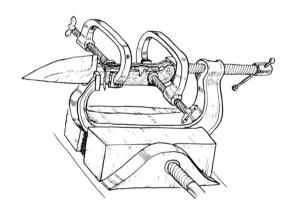

There are many brands and types of epoxy cement designed for a very wide variety of uses. Many knifemakers use an industrial-grade epoxy that is suitable for bonding wood to steel. You will have to contact an industrial supply house to find this. However, the color of these cements may be offensive, like steel grey or grey green. Find one that is clear.

I use a five-minute epoxy which is clear and can be found in most any hardware store. I have found it as strong for my use as industrial-grade epoxy, and nearly as heat-resistant. Don't get the bolster, shank, or rivets too hot while fairing down the handle because the glue's bond will be momentarily weakened, and could start to come apart. The epoxy hardens up again when it cools.

Fastening the Scales to the Shank

Now you know all that is necessary to affix the scales to the shank of your knife.

Wipe the glue surfaces off with acetone. Mix the epoxy thoroughly. Apply lightly to both surfaces and

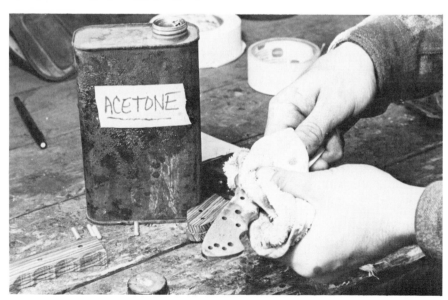

3. Cleaning off the tang with acetone.

4. Putting Vaseline on the ends of the slabs so that the epoxy won't stick there.

fill the insides of the holes in the shank which will form epoxy rivets. Coat the pins or rivets. Place the slabs against the shank and set the rivets or pins. Do not get any epoxy *inside* the female rivet or it may not compress properly and you will have a mess.

5. Here rubber gloves are used to keep the epoxy off the hands; however, I find that cumbersome. I use peanut oil on my hands instead and am very careful not to touch any of the glue surfaces with the oil.

6. Gluing all the surfaces and holes.

Tighten the clamps onto the handle. Go easy. If you have a bolster, start with the lengthwise clamp and snug the scales up against the bolster. Once the slabs are snugged up to the bolster, take the handle out of that clamp and press in the sides of the handle with three or four clamps, or you can leave it in *and* clamp it.

7. Putting in the pins.

8. Snugging up the bolster.

9. Undoing the snugger and
squeezing the slabs tightly
with the vise and clamps.

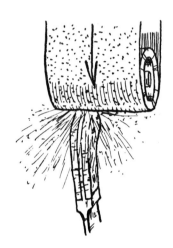

Epoxy should be squirting out from around the scales. Don't stop working on the clamping until it is set perfectly. And even then, keep your eye on it until the epoxy begins to set up, because the clamps can slip slowly out of position, pushing one or both of the scales out of alignment.

Shaping the Handle

The belt sander is the best tool for shaping the handle quickly. If you don't have a belt sander, you can use a rasp and sandpaper. Let's assume you have a belt sander.

Make the surface of the handle and the tops of the rivets flush. Do not take too much off the heads of the rivets. You will be going over them three or four more times, so leave enough meat on them to last through all these steps.

Do the rough shaping around the edges, forming the handle's silhouette and making the steel flush with the scales. Use a coarse-grit belt for these first shaping processes, say about a 36- or 40-grit. You'll probably develop many little tricks, as I have, in getting the relatively unsympathetic sander to produce graceful and sensitive handles.

Grinding off the tops of the pins against the flat belt backing keeps the side of the knife flat and even. Otherwise the wood between the pins tends to dish out during the shaping.

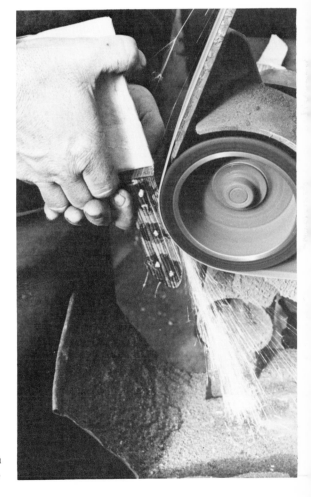

Beveling the wood and steel flush along the top of the handle.

Getting into the Tight Spots

The first thing you will notice after flattening out the most obvious high spots and rounding the butt corners is that the sander won't fit everywhere you want it to. Use your ingenuity and devise ways to reach these less-accessible areas. For example, if the blade or finger guard drops down at a 90 degree angle at the front of the handle, sand this part sideways, running the abrasive perpendicular to the wood grain. Do this as lightly and carefully as possible.

If you have a belt sander with a narrow belt, there may be a space where the belt is free from the metal backing. If so, this will be invaluable for finishing the underside of the handle. Another possibility for getting into tight areas is to use the overlapped belt technique described in the next section.

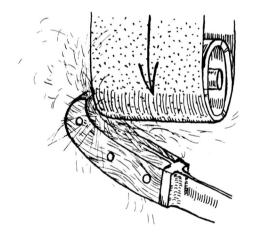

Making Finger Grips

If you want some nice rounded depressions for the fingers to grip, it would appear that this simply cannot be accomplished on the belt sander. Not true. The trick here is to let your belt run a little to one side of center so that it overlaps the platen. Then, take a piece of scrap iron and break down the stiffness of the overlapping section of the belt by forcing it (while the machine is running) to bend abruptly at one point.

Once the side of the belt has been softened up, use this overlapping belt area to reach in and bevel out finger grips and to shape nice curves in areas the sander wheel would not otherwise reach. Form the finger grips as neatly and precisely as possible. You want the depressions to be rounded but the ridges to be fairly well defined, not just lumps.

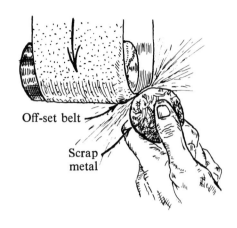

Off-set belt

Scrap metal

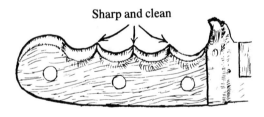

Sharp and clean

Which Grit Sizes?

Use the coarse-grit belt to do the rough shaping, then use progressively finer grits to finish and polish the handle, just as you did on the blade. I use belts that have become too worn to cut steel effectively, but that are still sharp enough to cut the wood.

I do the rough shaping with the 40-grit, following that with an 80-grit, a 120-grit, a 240-grit, and then finishing with a 240-grit on the flap sander.

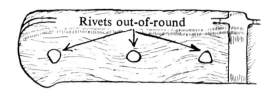

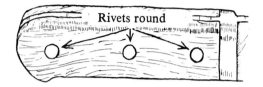

Grind the wood and the tops of the rivets or pins, as well as the bolster and butt plate, so they are a little more perfectly flush with each step. Remember, the rivet heads are very thin, so you don't want to take more off than you have to. You should end up with the rivet head and the surface of the handle perfectly even on about the 120-grit or 240-grit step.

The part of the handle where the rivets are must be flat, not round. If it is rounded you will take off the edge of the rivet head.

If the handle is set with pins, you don't have this problem, of course. You can bevel down the pin as much as you wish with no problem. One caution, though. Unless you have heat-resistant epoxy, do not get the pin too hot (over 200°F.) or the epoxy bond will be seriously weakened. Carefully finish all surfaces of the bolster, finger guard, or butt plate.

Finishing the Back of the Blade and the Bolster

As you go over the handle with progressively finer abrasives, go over the back of the blade also. Take it to a 240- or a 320-grit finish to buff for a mirror shine. Using the same fine belt, polish the bolster, as well as any other area that hasn't yet been finished.

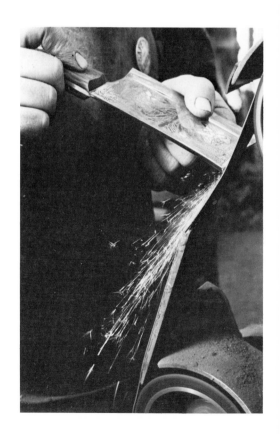

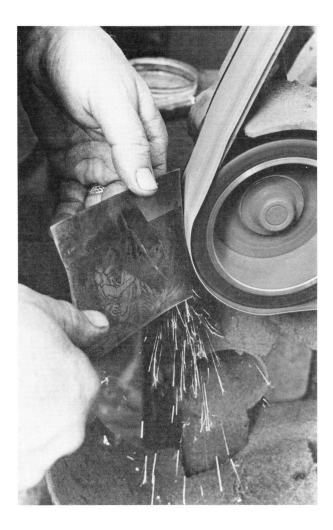

Finish the unsharpened edges of the blade. Give these areas a slightly rounded shape.

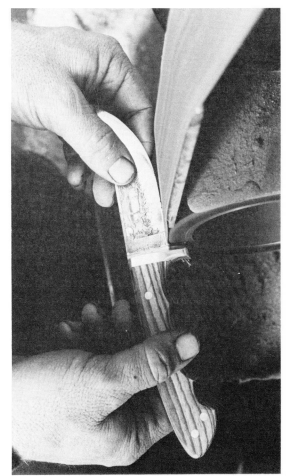

Wood Filler

The best wood filler, in case you ever do need to fill a small space or two, is made from epoxy glue and the sawdust from the wood you are using. Simply take a piece of the wood and grind it with a new, fine-grit belt, mix the dust half and half with mixed epoxy glue, and quickly press it into the crack. Or use a fine-grained commercially prepared wood filler, which has the advantage of being ready to use and is fast-drying, though rendering a dull, drab surface.

Healing Wood Checks and Hairline Cracks

Once upon a time, if I came to a minute check in the wood that would be a structural weakness or even a minor eyesore, I would remove the handle and make a new one. But now I use a miracle glue that is so runny it is absorbed into the most minute crack or check.

The glue, sold under the label Crazy Glue, dries as hard as epoxy glue and effectively removes small cracks and checks from the knife handle. It dries clear and the crack or check it absorbs into is invisible. Crazy Glue is the only modern adhesive I know of that has this particular absorbent characteristic.

Between the 90- and 120-grit sanding steps, I inspect all the edges of the handle, around the rivets or pins and any part that might contain the threat of a crack or check. Anything suspicious gets a drop of Crazy Glue. Then I just sand the glue residue flush during the 120-grit step.

Continue sanding the handle in finer grit steps, polishing up to a 240- or 320-grit. Buff the handle using the same stainless buffing compound that was used for the blade (See chapter 15, p. 183).

"Flap-sanding" the Handle

A Sandoflex sander or "flap-sander" is a revolving metal drum with a series of abrasive cloth flaps that strike the workpiece at high speed. Use it to sand the hollow areas of the handle. It imparts a very smooth finish to the handle, or with different types of abrasives it can produce different effects on the handle, such as driftwood or a raised grain effect. The flap-sander action is very much like the action of a sand blaster.

I use a 240-grit Sandoflex treatment following the 240-grit step on the belt sander, then follow up with the buffing step.

Danish Oil

After buffing the handle, I clean it and let a heavy coat of a Danish oil, such as Watco, soak into the wood, followed by a second coat in about a half hour. After this coat soaks in for half an hour, I wipe as much of the oil off as I can with a clean rag and let it dry overnight. This oil penetrates the surface of the wood and hardens, sealing it against moisture.

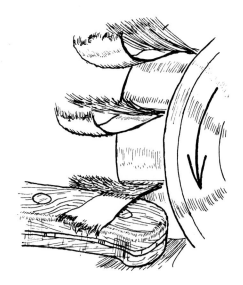

Flap-sanding the handle

Chapter 14

The Partial-tang One-piece Handle

A one-piece handle can be made from a piece of bone, horn, wood, or plastic. I would say that 95 percent of them are made out of stag antler. Let's assume that you are, in fact, making one out of a piece of stag antler.

Elk antler

Deer antler

Take a good look at your knife blade, consider the use you plan for it, and select the best piece of antler for your purpose. This most likely will be the butt end of an antler that is about 1 inch in diameter.

Hold the knife up to the antler and determine where to saw it off, and at what angle. Cut the antler, leaving an extra ¼ inch or so to play with. Now, with the belt grinder, carefully bevel off the end where it has been cut so that the antler will butt properly against the bolster.

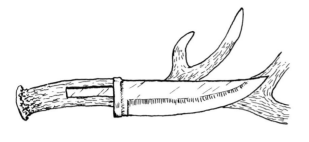

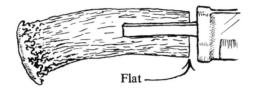

Flat

Select a drill bit that is about the same diameter as the tang. Grind down the tang to the size of the drill. Drill a hole into the antler to receive the partial tang. Drill this hole in the right spot on the antler, and at the proper angle. Put the handle on the blade. Does it fit all the way up to the bolster? You may need to redrill the handle or bevel off the tang. Make sure the hole is deep enough, but be careful not to drill through the side of the antler.

Carefully square off the end of the antler so it butts perfectly against the bolster. Bevel the bolster so it is flush with the antler. Precisely shape the finger guard.

Drill a series of $3/32$-inch holes on the inside of the bolster around the tang. These should be about ⅛ inch deep. These holes will fill with epoxy, forming rivets that will insure a practically unbreakable seal around the bolster.

Mix a sufficient amount of epoxy cement to fill the holes. Flow the cement into the hole in the handle. Be sure it flows all the way to the bottom—no

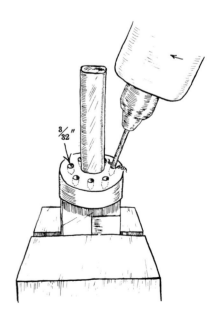

$3/32$″

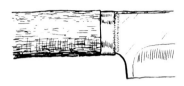

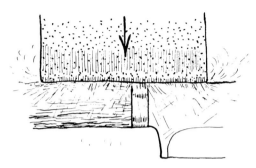

Grind handle and bolster flush

bubbles. Fill the little holes in the bolster. Coat the tang with epoxy, and fit the handle in place. Make sure the fit is perfectly snug and that the handle is turned in exactly the correct position.

Hold the knife together until the epoxy sets up. If you have set the handle with five-minute epoxy, you can hold it in your hands until the glue is firm. If you have used slower epoxy, place the knife handle in a vise, blade up, so the whole thing is balanced. Check the alignment every so often in case it drifts a little.

Finishing the Handle

Starting with a 120-grit belt, fair down the bone and brass until they are flush. Do not overheat the

epoxy. There should be no gap between the two materials.

It is a matter of personal taste as to how much of the antler is polished, and how much is left natural. I fair down the area near the bolster, and any sharp or uncomfortable protrusions. Otherwise, I leave the look of the handle as natural as possible.

Resand the handle to a 240-grit texture and then go over it with the "flap-sander."

The knife is now ready to polish. (See chapter 9.) Do not buff the bone with the same wheel that you buff the rest of the knife with. The dirt from the wheel will become gummed into the pores of the bone. Use a completely clean buffing wheel for the bone.

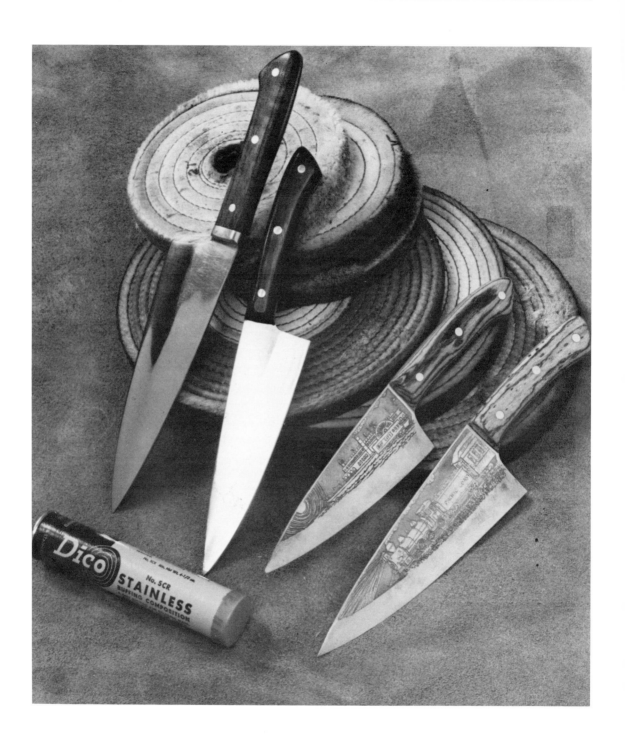

Chapter 15

Buffing the Knife

There are many kinds of buffing wheels available, composed of a wide variety of materials, such as flannel, abrasive-packed rubber, felt, metal brushes with compound in the bristles, et cetera. I have tried only flannel wheels, and I have found that hard flannel is best for knives.

You are ready to buff when you have the knife down to a pearly finish free of visible scratches. Use one, two, or three buffing wheels, depending upon how fine a finish you desire. As with the belt-sanding steps, each treatment cuts the surface with a progressively finer grit abrasive. The final buffing, where the actual shine is obtained, is called "coloring."

Good buffing can be accomplished in one step using "stainless" buffing compound, which comes in a white stick and is designed for buffing stainless steel. This is a fast-cutting compound, which nonetheless leaves a very bright shine on the work.

Buffing Safety

Start with either the blade or handle, it doesn't matter. This is one of the most hazardous steps in knifemaking. Buffing wheels are "grabby" and the blade can catch in the wheel and snap suddenly downward. Furthermore, the reflexive movements of the hand to retrieve the blade can add to the damage. I once cut myself across the knuckles, but it happened so fast that I can't tell how the knife got around to the other side of my hand. Most often it is the edge, tip,

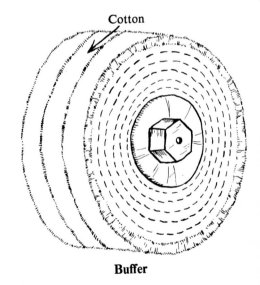

Cotton

Buffer

or back of the blade that will catch in the face of the wheel and shoot downward with amazing force, often tearing hunks of flannel from the wheel. It is better to sharpen the blade after buffing. Observe these precautions when buffing: Wear a heavy leather apron (buffing shops use chain-mail aprons); heavy, but not clumsy gloves; keep fingers above the knife so you don't lose one if the knife snaps downward; and watch carefully where the wheel is in relation to the top of the knife.

To prevent accidents, buff only the lower two-thirds of each side of the blade, then turn the knife around so the unbuffed side is along the bottom.

After you have buffed once, inspect for fine grinding lines that don't buff out. If necessary, retrace one or more of the belt-grinding steps to remove any unsightly grinder marks. Then, go over the blade one

Buffing the face of the blade of a small chef's knife.

Buffing the tight spots
where the underneath
of the handle comes
up to the blade.

more time so it is as clean as a mirror. Do not overheat
the cutting edge, since this could reduce the hardness.

When buffing the handle, don't bear down too
hard or you will burn the wood, plastic, or bone. If

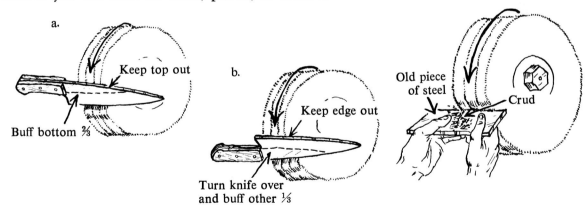

you find dirty compound piling up in certain areas of the handle, such as on the tang, buff in the direction of the belt-grinding marks, microscopic as they may appear. Use plenty of compound and the wheel will cut faster and cleaner. Again, if there are any grinder marks, go back a step or two and remove them.

Cleaning the Buffing Wheel

Remove the excess dirty compound. To do this, *carefully* press the side of an old dull knife blade into the face of the wheel, tilting the blade into the wheel so it skims off the old compound.

The side of the dropped edge on a chef's knife is another tricky spot to buff.

Chapter 16

Sharpening and Maintenance

For production work, I sharpen the knives in the following manner.

Forming the Burr

Form the edge evenly, using a 240-grit belt. Use light, even strokes across the whole blade with the edge downward at an 18- to 20-degree angle. After each stroke or two, turn the knife around and work on the other side of the blade. Work over the unsupported area of the belt, since this produces less friction heat and a more even edge.

The object is to form a visible burr along the entire length of the cutting edge. This shows that the blade is as sharp as you can get it on the 240-grit belt, and that there is uniform sharpness wherever the burr is visible. The burr forms because the steel at the very tip of the edge becomes so thin it finally becomes flaccid, like foil. At this point, abrasive will no longer cut

b.

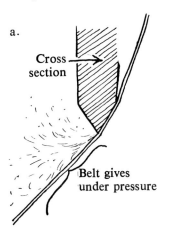

a.

Cross section

Belt gives under pressure

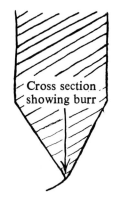

Cross section showing burr

a

b

c

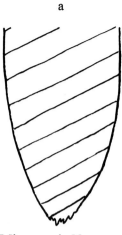

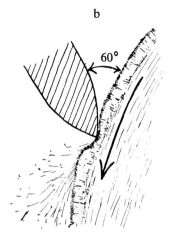

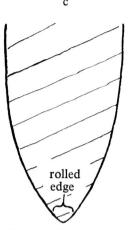

**Microscopic blow-up
of unstropped burr**

Angle of stropping

60°

rolled
edge

**Microscopic blow-up
of stropped cutting edge**

Beginning to buff the
burr off a utility
skinner.

it; it is simply bent over, and the thicker steel just beneath it is cut away, leaving the burr exposed.

I then repeat this operation, this time using a new 320- or 400-grit belt. It produces a finer, sharper, more polished edge, but does not remove the burr.

Stropping the Edge with the Buffer

The next step is to sharpen the blade on the buffer. Pass the edge of the blade across the face of the compound-loaded wheel at about two and one-half times the angle you used when you formed the burr. Continue this action back and forth on both sides of the edge until the burr is completely removed. Since the flannel threads of the buffing wheel are also flexible, they follow the burr around the microscopic edge of the knife and cut it away. The resulting edge is razor sharp, but more important, it is "stropped" by the action of the flexible threads of the buffing wheel

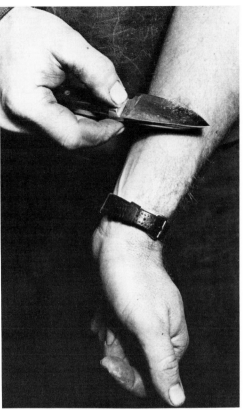

This is a demonstration people use. They say: "Look how sharp this blade is!" The trouble with this method is that you soon run out of arm hair and have to start on your legs.

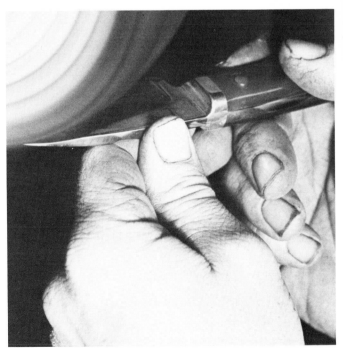

Working the tip.

so that the microscopic tip of the edge is rounded off; hence, at the microscopic level, the edge is blunt like a chisel. The chisel-edge resists stresses of all kinds. This edge is sharp enough to shave the hair off your arm and smooth enough to slide easily across your fingernail.

How to "See" the Sharpness

There are several ways to determine if an edge is sharp. Try cutting something, such as paper, rope, or cardboard. A simple and more sure-fire method is to look at it carefully. If the edge is the slightest bit dull, there will be a glint which is a reflection of light on the facet, which is the rounded edge. When the edge is perfectly sharp, there will be no visible glint, even when held opposite a strong light.

Hand-sharpening

A knifemaker should become expert in hand-sharpening. Not only will you need to sharpen in the field, but you will need to instruct your customers on the best ways to obtain a good edge quickly with hand tools.

Tools

A fine sharpening steel is a good tool for maintaining an edge. If the edge becomes dull and needs sharpening, use one or more clean, good-quality whetstones. The cheap varieties that are soft and porous are not good knife-sharpening tools. Higher quality carborundum stones with the smooth and coarse sides are good. Arkansas stones, similar to carborundum stones, come in a variety of grades, from coarse to exceedingly fine.

Cleaning the Whetstone

It is important to keep the stone clean. Periodically wash the stone with soap and water, or use a

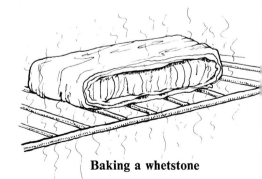

Baking a whetstone

solvent and a rag. Occasionally, it may be necessary to clean the pores of the stone if they are clogged up. To do this, soak the stone in kerosene, wrap tightly in a towel, and bake in a slow oven (250°F.).

Sharpening

Start with a coarse stone if the knife is very dull. Stroke evenly, keeping the angle to the stone constant. If the knife is used hard, sharpen at a slightly steeper angle, say, about 18 degrees for vegetable knives, 20 degrees for camping knives, 22 degrees for cleavers and hatchets. Take full, even strokes in either or both directions. Evenly hone all parts of the cutting edge. Don't hit the edge of the stone; a small chip in the edge may dull the knife. If

1. Working a fine edge on a utility skinner using a Washita stone. Also shown are three other types of sharpening stones.

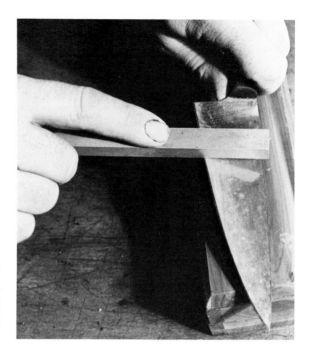

2. Bring up the edge on a small chef's knife with a small, square fine India stone. With a small stone, it is handier to hold the knife against a firm surface and move the stone across it.

3. Same operation, using a fine moonstone, which is actually hard porcelain.

4. Using a small porcelain rod. Available at a pottery-kiln store for just a few cents, this small rod will sharpen a blade as quickly and as keenly as a larger stone. Watch out you don't break one during use and cut your finger.

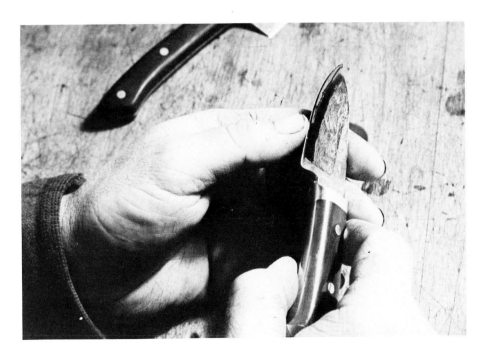

5. Feeling the edge with the thumb can tell you a little, but it is generally not a recommended test. To test sharpness, cut some leather, cardboard, paper, or rope. Or look at the edge as described in the text.

you press hard on the stone, without losing the proper angle, the knife will sharpen faster, getting just as sharp. Use a fine honing oil, or saliva, to keep the pores of the stone from clogging up, and wipe the surface of the stone frequently. Work from the coarser to the finer grit stones.

Stropping the Blade

After the blade is sharpened on the stone, it may be stropped. This further sharpens the edge and, more important, makes an edge that will last longer. The relatively soft stropping leather rounds the microscopic tip of the edge slightly, making it stronger, as well as bringing it to a finer point.

To strop the blade, rub some fine abrasive compound into the smooth side of a piece of a heavy leather strap, and work the blade, moving away from the edge.

Repeat this operation until the edge is fine and smooth enough to slide across your fingernail without the slightest tendency to catch. A stropped edge is a higher quality edge, and should be touched up occasionally on the strop, not on a steel or stone; otherwise, you will lose the microscopic rolled edge.

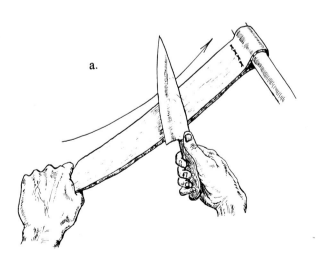

a.

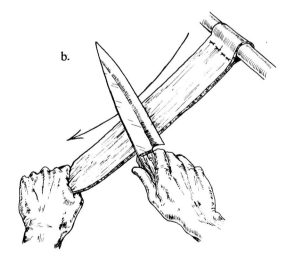

b.

Maintenance of the Knife

If the knives are made from old saw blades, they are high-carbon steel, and not stainless. Therefore, they are subject to discoloration and, if improperly cared for, corrosion and rust. Furthermore, if the handle is made from some organic material, such as wood or bone, this is also subject to decay. It is therefore important to take certain simple precautions. A knife will stand abuse for short periods of time, such as on backpacking trips or in a survival situation. But it should be well cared for most of the time.

First, the knife should be kept clean and dry. It can be washed with warm water and soap or mild detergent if necessary. Preferably, the knife will simply be wiped clean with a damp cloth. Occasionally, it should be lightly oiled on both the handle and blade. Any oil will do for the knife, but if it is used for food preparation, it is best to use vegetable, olive, or mineral oil. It may be harmful to the handle and the blade to leave the knife setting in dishwater or in a damp place. Rinse the knife with fresh water after exposure to salt water. The luster can be returned to tarnished carbon steel by hand polishing with certain compounds, such as powdered copper cleaner. There are a number of such compounds on the market. Or, you can rebuff the knife periodically, which should make it look exactly like new.

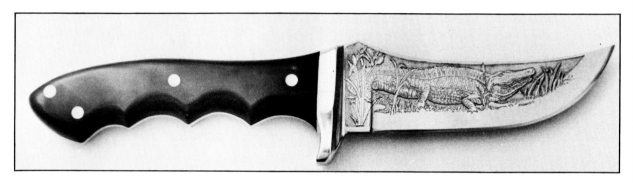

A 5-inch skinner with black buffalo horn handle.
Crocodile etching is by Jessie Oster.

Chapter 17

Step-by-Step Checklist

Each step in knifemaking should follow the last as a natural progression of growth. If the pattern of activity is disharmonious, the knife will suffer. Therefore, try to develop a rhythm in your work. Build a process that is one continuous growth, from the beginning to the finished knife.

Obviously, there are many ways and methods to make knives. What I have presented is one approach. Whatever methodology you use, conceive of an even, step-by-step flow of treatments to the materials and you will maximize the amount of stored energy within the structure that you build.

Here is a list of the treatments for building a knife with *full-tang scale handle* and a *brazed bolster*. I chose this handle type because it is the most complicated. If you are making a partial-tang one-piece handle, you can use this list. Simply skip the steps that do not apply.

Step-by-Step Order of Process for Full-tang Handle with Brass Bolster

1. Design the knife and make a silhouette on posterboard. 58.
2. Select and prepare the steel. 14–16, 61.
3. Trace the silhouette onto the steel. 61–62.

4. Cut out the knife. 63–65.
5. Trim and shape the silhouette with a grinder. 65–66.
6. Grind the cutting edge. 71–76.
7. Regrind the edge and sides of the blade with a belt grinder, using 40- and 80-grit abrasive. Refine the silhouette. 76–77.
8. Design and cut out the brass pieces. 79–82.
9. Cut out the notches to receive brass fill. 82–83.
10. Braze on the bolster. 86–91.
11. Fair down the brass, clean up the blade, and shape the bolster. 91–96.
12. Straighten the blade. 67, 123–26.
13. Harden the blade by heating to critical temperature and then quenching. 105–17.
14. Test hardness with a file and the belt grinder. 115, 119–20.
15. Clean the surface with a worn abrasive belt. 134.
16. Temper the blade to the desired color hardness. 116–17.
17. Anneal the back of the blade and the tang. 117–19.
18. Using the belt grinder, test the hardness again. 119–20.
19. Straighten the blade again. 123–26.
20. Regrind the edge with a new 40-grit belt or a water-cooled grinder. 129–30.
21. Regrind the entire blade with five or six progressively finer polishing steps, from 80- to 600-grit. 130–34.
22. Etch the blade, if desired. 211–26.
23. Drill the rivet holes. 137–40.
24. Carefully clean the handle area and the inside of the bolster. 158.
25. Trace and cut the handle slabs on the band saw. 157.
26. Shape the front of the handle to precisely fit against the bolster. 160–61.

27. Check the fit between the scales and the tang. Straighten the tang, if necessary. 158–59.

28. Clamp one slab at a time onto the tang and drill out the rivet holes for the metal and epoxy rivets. 161–62.

29. If you are using rivets, not pins, countersink the holes in the slabs to accommodate the rivet heads. 146–47.

30. Modify the rivets or make the pins from brazing rod. 143–46.

31. Check C clamps and practice clamping the handle. 163.

32. Mix and apply epoxy cement. 163–64.

33. Install rivets or pins and set the clamps. 164–68.

34. After removing clamps, roughly shape the handle and bolster with a coarse abrasive belt. 168.

35. Resand the handle with an 80-grit belt and minutely shape the bolster/finger guard and finger grips, if any. 170–72.

36. Fill any cracks or checks with Crazy Glue. 174.

37. Resand the handle and bolster with a 120- and then a 240-grit belt. 174.

38. Finish the back of the blade, bringing it flush with the top of the bolster. 172.

39. Sand the handle and the bolster with a 240-grit flap-sander. 174.

40. Buff the entire knife. 174–75.

41. Put the final edge on the knife with a 240- and a 320-grit belt. 189–91.

42. Buff the edge to razor sharpness. 191.

43. Apply Danish oil to the handle. 175.

44. Clean the etching and remove all buffing compound from the handle. 224.

45. Inspect the entire knife and bring it all up to par.

46. Sign the knife.

David, Francine, and Dennis behind our knife display.

Chapter 18

Production Notes

Mass versus Individual Production

The attitude of the worker is different if he or she is attempting to make a large number of knives to furnish some portion of his or her livelihood than if he or she is making only a few knives. The person in business must develop additional techniques and skills if he or she is going to maintain high quality and loving grace in the craftsmanship while still producing enough knives to support himself or herself. In this chapter are some ideas that should enable the craftsman to come a little nearer to this goal.

I have found methods to organize my work flow so that the individual and production aspects of the process enhance each other. For example, I may cut out a large number of blades in one day—each one individually. I think the individuality of each knife is somewhat enhanced because I can get "into" the design aspect of knifemaking in this manner. Each time I repeat the process I go more deeply into that aspect of myself from which the action emerges. The action or technique is repeated and deepened, uninterrupted by the frequent stops and breaks necessary when making one knife at a time.

To me, it is obviously more efficient both in physical and psychic energy terms to produce knives in batches, rather than individually. If you just make one knife at a time, you have to go around to a different machine each time you take the next step. If you need to change grit sizes on the belt, you have to turn off the machine, make the change, and turn it on again. You have to think about it each time, and this also takes energy. But when you work in batches, you work without interruption, saving wear and tear on the equipment and yourself. You can relax more, because you get into the swing of a given process; you can continue until you really start getting tired of it, and then you can move on to another step.

So we don't need to worry that if we produce a large number of knives, we will necessarily lose the personalized qualities of the handmade knives.

Developing a Relationship with Your Tools

The necessary shop layout and equipment have been discussed in the chapter about tools, so I won't go into much depth here, except for special or modified tools for faster production. Your desire to make good knives, the very creative impulse, is channeled through you to the knifework via the tools. If your tools are a poor channel, then the output· in terms of work and knives will reflect this. Tune in to each of your machines, and listen to them deeply. Close your eyes and listen. Does the tool sing when it runs, or does it whine or growl? Of all the things that you can do for your tools, good listening is perhaps the most important. The sound is a series of layered vibrations, rhythms, and harmonies, and through this current of sound you can enter into your machine and become one with it. It may be hard to believe, but I am convinced that with this form of machine communication, you can not only diagnose your machine's ills, but detect a deeper harmony of life within the machine, which can manifest as a surprising degree of subtle cooperation.

That's right! I said that your machines will cooperate with you if you listen to them. Ask an old machinist if it isn't true.

The Strategy

To get started on a production run, I cut out quite a number of blades at one time. If I am using saw-blade steel, I use a cutting torch and cut up an entire length (say 6 feet) of saw blade at one time. Using templates, I just trace the knives out with chalk, or in a smoked surface, a little larger than I want them to be when they are done. I draw them, if possible, so that two knives will have a common edge and there is a little less cutting to do. I draw them as closely fitting as possible to save steel. These may either be traced from a template, or drawn free-hand. In the long run, it is best to use templates. This way, you can always draw out the best shapes, eliminating the dogs before they are manifested.

To clean up the rough edges, I use one of my least-favorite grindstones because this operation uses up the stone fast and is not as exacting as grinding the edge. Specifically, I use the big, thick, heavy stones for cleaning up the silhouettes. For grinding the edges I use stones about 1¼ inch in thickness.

Having cut all the knives out in one operation and shaped all the silhouettes in the second operation, I now install the special adjustable pressure brace onto the work rest of the grinder and grind all the edges. Sometimes I don't use the pressure brace for blades of 1½ inches or less, but guide these with my hands. I am careful not to grind any knives so thin that they will warp, knowing that I can safely regrind them after tempering, using either a new 80-grit belt or a water-cooled grinder.

I wear gloves so that I can continue grinding even after the blade gets hot, and so that if I slip, I will grind away part of the glove, instead of my finger. I wear a respirator when grinding and when doing the initial sanding steps on the handles. I have a bucket of water right by the grinder so I can instantly cool the blade anytime I want to check it with my fingers. This is a fast, rough grinding step.

After going through all the knives that I have cut out, I then straighten them on the anvil, and go over them again on the stone, this time very carefully.

Blades that will be thinly ground, such as chef's knives, are ground as fine as possible without danger of warpage. You will have to learn from experience just how fine that is on each type of knife.

Now, I regrind them again, this time more carefully, using a 36-grit belt on the small belt grinder. Since the wheel is of a much smaller diameter, I can make the hollow grinds more pronounced.

Then, I braze on any brass pieces, if any are called for, and then clean up the brazing.

Using an electric kiln, I heat up to five knives simultaneously, to a full, red glow. I quench them in olive oil, one at a time, holding them on the handle area with tongs.

I clean them off with an old 80-grit belt so they are nice and shiny, and draw them to the desired color in the kitchen oven. I use a flat cookie sheet, but do not allow the edges to rest flat down on the bottom of the sheet. Have them suspended just above the surface of the sheet, on another flat piece of metal, or they will heat unevenly. I temper about twenty-five or thirty blades at one time this way. It takes some practice, however, to get them all perfectly evenly done at once. You may have to take them out individually as they reach a particular color-hardness.

Each time I do a step, I do it to every knife in the batch. Then the handles and the backs of the knives are annealed, and the knives are straightened on the anvil. I don't strive to get them perfectly straight at this point, but just so they look and feel straight.

Regrinding After Tempering

Now the blades are reground according to the particular design-needs of the individual knife. If it is

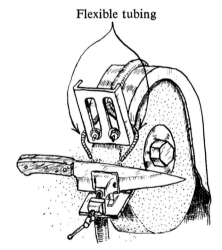

Flexible tubing

Water-spray attachment for keeping blade cool

to be a fairly thick-bladed knife, then it is probably ready to be taken through the six polishing steps using grit sizes 80 through 600. If it is to be a very fine-bladed knife, then further grinding will inevitably be necessary after tempering. In my shop, this may be done on the same grinding machine, but with a water-spray cooling device in action, or it may be done on the water-cooled belt grinder. A fine, light spray of cold water is directed at the workpiece where it comes in contact with the abrasive. This way there is little chance of overheating the hardened blade. The tempered blades can be reground without a coolant bath, but it is slow and painstaking for production work. Another advantage is that the water removes most of the dust, producing a cleaner, healthier shop environment.

Water-cooled Belt Grinder

After the knife is properly reground against the stone, I begin to work the blade with a water-cooled belt grinder. This machine has an attachment which directs a fine spray of water against the surface of the moving belt. It is a 2-inch by 48-inch three-wheel belt grinder. I modified this machine for knifemaking by moving the work wheel out further to provide better clearance underneath it.

As the belt spins around, excess water flies off and is trapped by the metal cowling, but the surface of the belt remains wet. This lubricates the cutting action and cools the workpiece. This speeds the grinding without generating heat in the blade. The grinding is done exactly as described earlier in the book, except the danger of heating the blade is eliminated.

There are disadvantages to a water-cooled belt sander. First, waterproof belts cost about 40 percent more than the nonwaterproof belts. However, ordinary resin belts can tolerate a certain amount of water spray on the surface, but not on the back. A light mist on the surface is adequate to prevent the

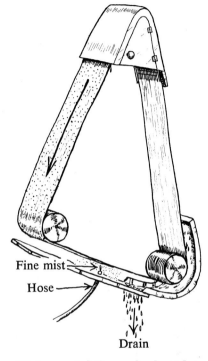

Fine mist

Hose

Drain

Water-cooled three-wheel sander

knife from overheating during the polishing process.

Second, the water-spray arrangement is somewhat difficult to set up. You have to have piped-in water that runs out the drain, leaving only the cooled workpiece and the water bill. Or, you have to make a reciprocating, filtered system. If you don't know what that is, maybe you aren't ready for it. It consists of a reservoir of water, a pressure pump to deliver the spray, pans to collect the water after it has been used, and filters to clean it. It also needs constant additions of water, since some water is lost through misting and evaporation, not to mention leaks.

Francine giving a final polish and inspection to a batch of assorted knives.

A third disadvantage is that a water-cooled machine, any water-cooled machine, is cold and messy to operate.

However, if you are serious about knife production—that is, you want to eliminate the main hassles between you and smooth productive knifemaking—the advantages of water-cooled machines well overbalance their problems.

Oil-cooled Belt Grinder

Another possibility for keeping the workpiece cool, although one which I haven't tried, is to use oil as a coolant. The advantage here is that you can use ordinary resin belts, not waterproof belts, saving 40 percent on belt costs.

Oil is more difficult to apply—at least you need a pressurized reciprocating filtered system. Furthermore, the oil spray is dangerous to your health and is a potential fire hazard. Use a light cutting oil with a very high flashpoint to minimize this danger.

If you don't have a liquid-cooled sander, here are some tips on the grinding-polishing steps using dry abrasives. Use your very newest belts to grind the edges of the knife. After they have lost their initial super sharpness, don't use them for tempered edges anymore. Use them for the sides of the blades, and then finally to shape the handles. If you use a new belt to grind handle material, such as wood, bone, or Micarta, the belt will load up, becoming useless before it is worn out. So, get the belt practically worn out on steel first, then let it fill up with handle material.

Building a Stock of Blades

Have a large stock of finished blades on hand. When a customer wants a knife, he or she can choose a blade that suits his or her fancy, and have the knife in reasonably short order.

Chapter 19

Etching Designs into the Steel

The beauty of a knife may be greatly enhanced by etching designs or scenes into the blade. This is done prior to putting on the handle, by coating the entire knife with a specially prepared wax, scraping the design into the wax with an etching tool or "burin," and then dipping the blade into a tank of strong acid until the design is deeply etched. This is an ancient method of beautifying metals, glass, and other materials, and when properly executed will greatly enliven and enhance the appearance of the knife.

Preparing the Surface of the Blade

To prepare the surface to be etched, grind it completely smooth and free of pits and blemishes, polish it to a satin finish, and buff it. Bring the blade to a 600-grit finish before buffing. The etching should be the *last* thing done to the shank prior to fitting the handles.

Applying the Wax

Wash the blade with cleanser, or clean with acetone, and then coat the entire surface, including the handle area, with etching resist or "ground." This is prepared from equal parts of powdered asphaltum and melted beeswax. See your local art supply store for these materials. Melt the beeswax in a saucepan, slowly stirring in an equal amount by weight of asphaltum. This does not double the volume in the pan, but adds about a third to a half.

Allow the ground to cool, and then break into small chunks. Heat the blade over a stove burner or hot plate and rub the resist onto the blade. The blade should be hot enough to get a smooth thin coating over the entire surface, but not so hot as to burn the resist or remove the hardness of the blade. If the resist smokes, it has probably become too brittle and you should rewax the blade. Allow the blade to cool by hanging it from a clothespin. Be sure the entire surface is covered, including the areas you do not expect to immerse in the acid bath, because even the fumes from the acid bath have etching properties.

The Etching Tool

If you plan to do a lot of etching, get at least one good etching burin, since your ability to clearly inscribe the design into the wax is limited by the tool. You can make fine little microscopic scraping tools of various shapes out of round carbon steel stock, like automobile push rods or ¼-inch round files. Use the belt grinder to remove stock in the appropriate places. Harden and temper to a light straw color so the tool will hold its edge while being scraped against the knife steel.

For fine detail make a wooden handle the size of a pencil, with a needle epoxied into a small hole in the end. Some people use a needle or pin stuck into a pencil eraser, but you can do better than that.

There are a variety of etching tools at your local art supply store, but the ones we have tried seem a little clumsy.

Cutting the Artwork into the Wax

If you use the beeswax-asphaltum ground, inscribe the artwork either in the warm sunshine, or under a strong, hot light bulb, so that the wax is warm and pliable. Otherwise it is difficult to cut away the

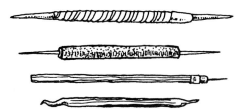

Types of burins

wax, and it has a tendency to crack away from the blade. Warm and flexible wax is a pleasure to work with, especially if it has been coated thinly and evenly onto the blade. Let it warm up before you begin your artwork. Don't get it too warm, or the wax will become sticky, making it hard to get clean lines.

A large magnifying glass, mounted on a stand, helps achieve minute detail in etching. The one Francine Martin is using in the picture has a paper shade taped onto it to cut out the glare from the light. Magnifying goggles that are worn by some jewelers serve the same purpose.

Make the designs clean, centered or balanced, and complete. Follow the lines of the knife. Use contrasts of detail and blocks. You can find many ideas for etching subjects and techniques at the local library, especially in children's books. The etching looks more sculptural if the background is etched out, as opposed to simple line drawings. Be sure to get through the wax, clear down to the steel, even in the fine lines and in the midst of great detail.

That thing in front of Francine's face is a magnifying glass with a paper shade to reduce the glare from the light bulb.

An etcher's-eye view of a waxed blade. First she starts with the outline of the major forms in the piece, then takes out the background as she works in the detail.

Using the Acid Bath

Here comes the tricky part. You will have to experiment quite a bit before you can get a clear, well-defined bite on a regular basis. Part of the problem is that very few people in this country etch in steel, so there aren't many books which contain any detailed information on the subject. Another complexity is that all the knife steels are different, and the acid influences them in subtly different ways. I have found that there are so many factors that influence the type of bite you get, all interacting with one another, that you really must have experience with a capital E before you can be assured of consistent results.

Giving the areas where the wax is thin an extra coat. This is a very important step because any weak areas in the wax, including nicks and scratches, can result in deep bites into the side of the cutting edge and the borders of the etching.

Before you immerse the wax-coated, designed blade into the acid, make sure there are no nicks or scratches in the ground anywhere outside the area to be etched. The wax tends to get very thin along the edges of the blade. Cover these areas with an extra layer of ground just prior to immersing it in the acid. To do this, melt a piece of ground material in a small pot or can and then paint this onto the *slightly warmed* blade along areas where the ground looks suspiciously thin or nicked.

Mixing the Acid

The basic acid used to bite steel is called Aqua Regia and consists of three or four parts muriatic (hydrochloric) acid to one part nitric acid. This is the famed "royal water" and is (or was) the only known acid that will dissolve gold. You can get muriatic acid at swimming pool supply houses, and nitric acid at chemical houses, or possibly at a photo-engraving shop.

Before you mix any acid, consider a few safety precautions. Any acid is *very* dangerous, and Aqua Regia is particularly dangerous. Always mix and use the acid outdoors, never indoors, unless you have a chemical laboratory with a powerful fume hood. Always stand upwind of the acid because the fumes are very potent and can damage your lungs.

Always have running water and baking soda on hand in case you need to flush and neutralize acid that has splashed on you. But do not pour water or baking soda into the acid bath; it could explode. (Never add water to acid, only acid to water, and very slowly.)

Wear goggles and a chemical mask when working with the acid.

And finally, when you are finished with a batch of acid, don't pour it down the drain or in the toilet unless you want to commit hari-kari. Dig a large hole in

Three knives ready for the acid bath.

the ground away from people, plants, and animals, and use that as a vat to neutralize the acid with baking soda and water. What a hassle. Probably your local firehouse can help you in safely disposing of the acid, but perhaps their method isn't any better than the one described above. Good luck.

I have heard of a number of different combinations of Aqua Regia, with water or additional hydrochloric acid added to the basic three-to-one Aqua Regia mixture. However, we have obtained the sharpest, cleanest bites, with the least lifting of the ground, with straight Aqua Regia that has been aged one month. When you mix the two acids together, a chemical change occurs, as evidenced by prolonged bubbling and a change of color from clear to a maple-syrup gold. If you use the acid while it is still "green," you may find that the bite is very fast, but that the ground lifts even faster, resulting in a too-shallow, perhaps even illegible etching.

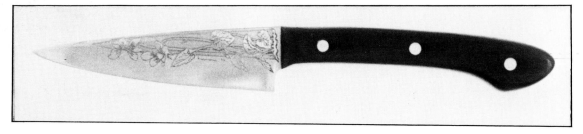

A cleanly bitten but too shallow etching in a paring knife. If the blade had been left in the acid longer, the bite would have been deeper, but the ground would have lifted around some of the detail, ruining the etching. The acid was too fresh.

The nice thing about fresh acid—that is, acid that you begin using after one month of aging—is that the bite, though shallow, is very clean. Every detail will be bitten perfectly, and the background will be absolutely free of blemishes. The knives shown have been bitten to a good depth, with clear backgrounds and good detail.

Closeup of *Cosmic Lady* showing a clean, even bite and a clear background.

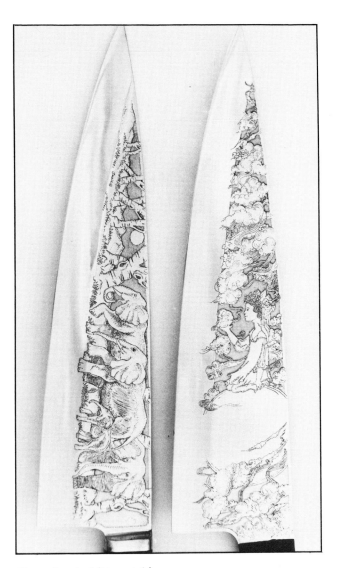

Two cleanly bitten etchings on 10-inch chef's blades. *Elephant Herd* by Jessie Oster and *Cosmic Lady on Small Planet* by Joyce Sierra.

Seven-inch chopping knife with *Brown Pelican* etched by Francine Martin.

Detail of *Pelican*. In the background you can see the striations and granular microstructure of the steel.

After you have bitten, say, about 100 knives with a batch of two gallons, you will notice some funny things happening in the background of your etchings. At first they will show a beautiful quilting effect. As you continue to use the bath, the background will begin to show blotches and bubbles. Furthermore, as the acid begins to become too old it will pit the background somewhat, and the more you use the acid, the worse the problem becomes.

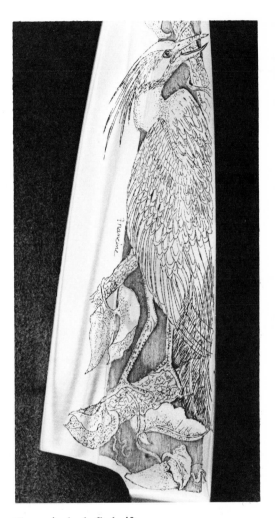

Seven-inch chef's knife with *Heron* by Francine Martin.

As the acid is used over and over, the quality of the background begins to change. At first there is a beautiful, gentle quilting effect as shown in the background of *Plantain* by Francine Martin.

The background of this etching, *Lady Picking Apples*, is deeply pitted in several places.

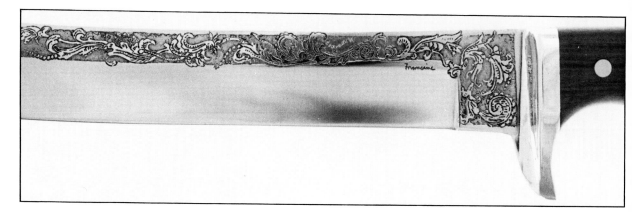

Detail of carving knife shown at the beginning of the
chapter. Note the slightly mottled background, the
harbinger of worse things to come.

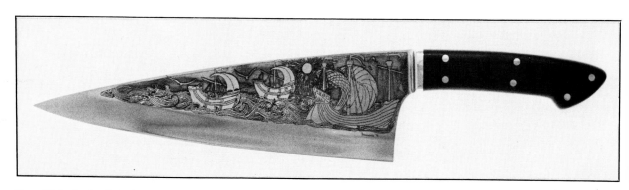

Two 10-inch chef's knives etched by Francine Martin.
Note the blackened areas in the background. Again, the
acid is too old, causing thousands of microscopic pits
to form.

The Temperature of the Acid Bath

The acid should be slightly above room temperature when etching, say about 70° to 75°F. Otherwise the bite is too slow, and the ground could lift before the bite is deep enough. You can warm up the acid with a light bulb shining into the bath from above.

Notice that as you use the bath, the temperature increases due to the action of the acid. If you bite a number of knives on the same afternoon, you may find that the temperature has increased, and with it the intensity of the acid bite. It is easy to ruin a knife by having the acid too hot. I had the experience of having acid so hot that it melted the wax on the blade. As soon as the ground melted, of course, the surface area to be etched increased greatly. With that, the amount of activity in the tank increased, and the ferocity of the action too, causing further increase in temperature, and so on. Needless to say, there wasn't much left of the knife by the time I returned. But that was back in the trial and error days.

If etching outdoors, you can adjust the temperature of the bath by placing it either in the sun or the shade, depending upon the temperature of the air. Basically, this means in the sun on cool days and in the shade on warm days. If it is a cool day with no sun, or if you are etching at night, use a light bulb, or perhaps even a heat lamp shining down into the bath.

Light

This is an unexpected variable. We have found on a number of occasions that a very uneven bite corresponded with uneven lighting—where part of the etching was in the shade and the other part in strong light. We have concluded that the light stimulates the action, and that therefore it should be constant across the surface of the etching.

The Bath

The best position for the knife is flat in a pan with the etching facing up. We tried etching in a vertical position, but ran into trouble, especially with knives that have bolsters. When the bubbles given off by the action rise, they naturally follow the surface of the blade. They tend to agitate the section of the etching across which they travel, causing this section to bite faster.

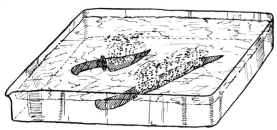

Etching knives horizontally

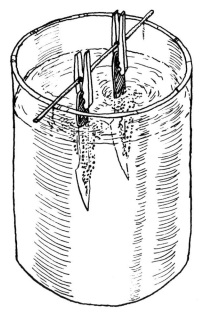

Glass container with knives suspended by clothespins slipped onto a metal rod

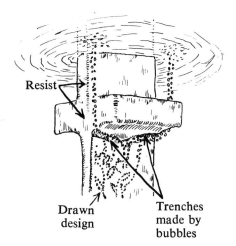

Resist

Drawn design

Trenches made by bubbles

Under-acid view of vertically suspended knife with bolsters

Biting the Knife

After double-checking for unwanted nicks, scratches, and thin spots in the ground, slip in the blade, etching up. About every ten minutes or so take out the knife and carefully inspect it. Brush out the etching with a fairly soft acid brush, or a large feather. This brushing action swabs out the residue caused by the chemical action, leaving a clear avenue of communication between the steel and the acid.

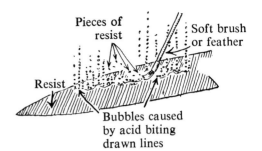

Inspecting and cleaning the etching every five to ten minutes makes for an even bite and guarantees that the wax will not lift unnoticed.

Humpback Whale, **etching by** Francine Martin on a 2-inch dropped-edge utility skinner with a buffalo-horn handle.

Experience will tell you when the etching is ready, since the time depends on several factors that vary constantly. These are: the temperature of the acid bath, the strength of the acid, the amount of etching activity in the tank, and the amount of light. The higher the temperature, the faster it bites. The more the acid is used, the weaker it becomes. The more surface being etched in the tank, the higher the rate of activity, and the faster it will bite.

The etching should be noticeably cut out when it is ready. If you are not sure, after examining it carefully, touch a spot very carefully with a sharp tool to determine if there is enough depth to the etching. If the ground is starting to lift, this is a good time to call it quits and scrape off the wax. The best tool to use for removing the wax is a rotating wire brush on the grinding arbor.

Multilayer Etching

It is possible to do a two- or even a three-layer etching that makes the design stand in complete sculptural relief. It is done by etching away part of the design, and then "stopping out" areas which you want to be more shallow. Stop out an area by washing the knife with water, warming it slightly under the bulb, and then painting liquid resist in the areas you want to be more shallow. Then rebite the blade in the acid.

The effect of shadowy areas in the background is achieved by scraping away certain areas of the ground between bites in the acid. If you want a highly reliefed figure in the foreground, and another figure in a shadowy background, you would stop out the foreground figure and scrape the ground away from the background figure, and then rebite in the acid.

Artwork

Traditionally, the subjects used to adorn knives have been somewhat limited in their scope. Most commonly the subjects have included hunting scenes, scenes from wars and famous fights, nudes, and scrollwork. Famous historical personages and events are also favorite topics.

We have had a very positive response from etching nearly anything that is beautiful and meaningful on a blade. It has surprised us to find people just as appreciative of an etching of some flower or herb as they are of a hunt scene. People can appreciate fine artwork on the side of a knife blade as well as anywhere else. Therefore, the acceptance of the design comes as a result of good craftsmanship and artistic and symbolic good taste.

In the photos of some of our etchings, observe, if you will, the use of space, the juxtaposition of detail and blocks of open spaces, and the wide variety of subject matter. Perhaps of highest importance is the

Rabbit in Woods, etching by Joyce Sierra on a chef's knife.

way an etching works with a blade—how the movement in the design harmonizes with the movement in
the knife itself.

Lady with Grapes, etching by Francine Martin on a chef's knife.

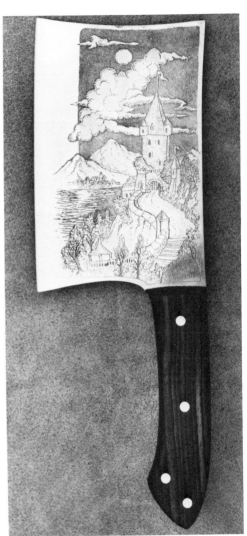

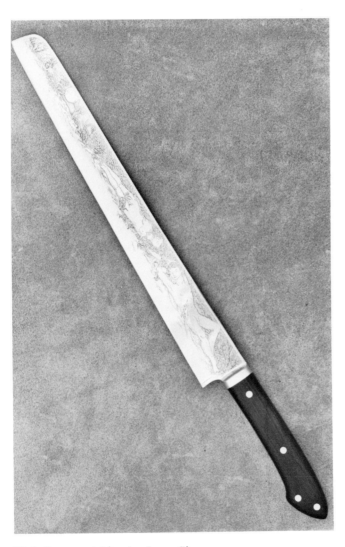

Castle, etching by Jessie Oster
on a 5-inch chopping knife.

Nude Lovers, etching by Joyce Sierra
on a 9-inch slicing knife.

Elf and Spider Drinking Tea,
etching by Jessie Oster on
a chef's knife.

Moonlit Lovers, etching by Andra Rudolf
on a 7-inch Chinese-style chopping knife.

Pan, etching by Joyce Oster.

Pair of Peacocks,
etching by Francine Martin.

Fairy Child, etching by Joyce Sierra on a 6-inch chef's knife.

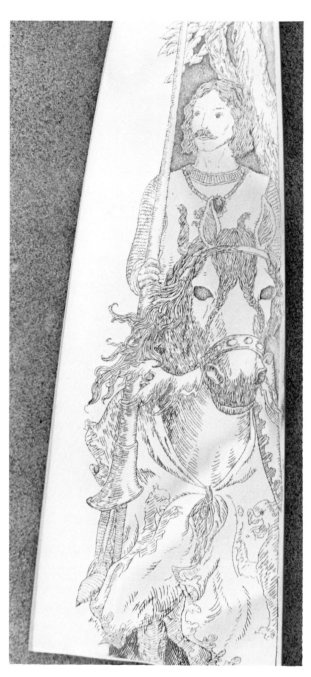

Knight and Horse, etching by Joyce Sierra.

Three dropped-edge utility knives. *Horse*, etching by Joyce Sierra; *Whale* and *Rabbit*, etchings by Francine Martin.

Chapter 20

Sheathmaking

I use three basic types of sheaths for my knives. Short knives without finger guards, such as my favorite utility design, are usually fitted with some form of pouch sheath. With this type there is no snap. It is form-fitted and the knife fits snugly into the sheath, held in place by the pressure of the leather against the handle.

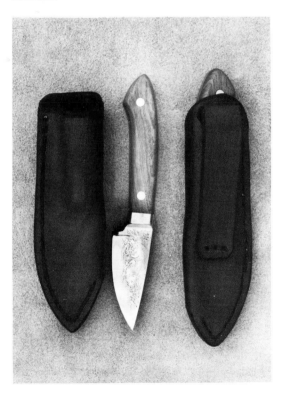

Front and rear views of two pouch sheaths.

Front and rear of two snap-pouch sheaths.

If the knife has a finger guard, the pouch is modified so it will open at the top of the blade case with a snap. This sheath is also molded around the knife.

If the blade is curved backwards, as with some of the more radical skinners, a molded sheath is difficult to make, and we usually resort to a more traditional flat snap-type sheath.

Of course, there are many variations of these and other types of sheaths. Perhaps, after reading this chapter, you will use these techniques to make a sheath of some other design.

I will show you how to make the traditional snap sheath and the pouch sheath with the use of a few simple drawings. Then I will show you our method of making the snap-pouch (snouch) sheath with the use of photos of Roger Withrow making one.

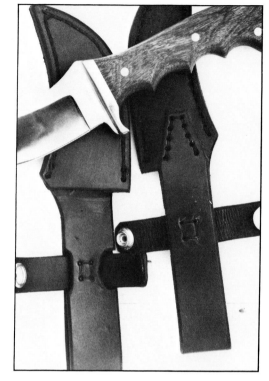

Front and rear of two traditional snap sheaths.

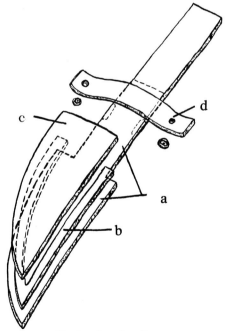

Parts of a sheath

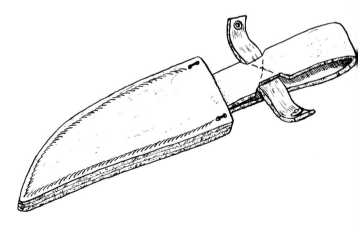

I recommend that you read the entire chapter before you try to make any of the types of sheaths because the techniques for all three types are very similar, and the photos and drawings each bring a different quality of information to bear on the problem.

Making a Snap Sheath

Let's look at a snap-type sheath and its component parts. The sheath is made of good quality, heavy (7- to 8-ounce) oak- or French-tanned leather.

First, cut out the main piece (**a**) that forms the body of the sheath, i.e., the back section and the belt loop. Place the knife on the leather and trace the outline ⅜ inch wider than the knife on all sides. Make the belt loop extend twice the length of the handle plus ¾ inch. Cut out this piece.

Draw out the front piece (**c**) in exactly the same manner. Carefully scribe the top where the blade will rest so that the blade and the sheath fit together snugly. Cut this piece out.

On a piece of leather slightly thinner than the blade, trace out the spacer (**b**). Use the blade as a template for the inside line and the frontpiece to trace the outside line.

Make the snap strap (**d**). This piece should be proportional in size to the mass of the knife. A little snap strap would look skimpy on a large knife, and a little knife would be lost under a big strap. Draw out and cut this strap about 1½ inches longer than the diameter of the handle.

Next, using an edge beveler, round off the edges of the belt loop strap, the snap strap, and the top of the front piece.

Don't position the snap strap too close to the top of the front piece or it may be cut by the blade. Don't position the snap strap too high on the belt loop since it won't hold the blade in well. Determine a good

Beveling the sheath's edges

position for the snap strap on the belt loop. Cut notches on (a) so that the snap strap will bend comfortably around the belt loop and the handle of the knife.

Using leather dye, stain all the leather parts except where they will be glued. The dye reduces the effectiveness of the leather cement. These areas are: where the belt loop joins onto the main body of the sheath, the areas around the blade case, and where the snap strap is connected. Allow the dye to dry thoroughly before resuming work on the sheath.

Now you are going to sew, not rivet, the belt loop to the back of the body of the sheath. If you were to use rivets, the handle would abrade against the rivet heads. This produces dents and brassy lines on the handle. To properly sew the belt loop, the stitching should be slightly inset into the leather so the blade

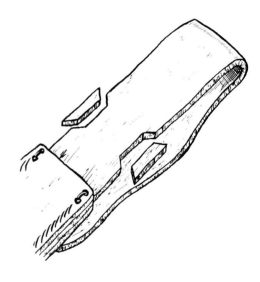

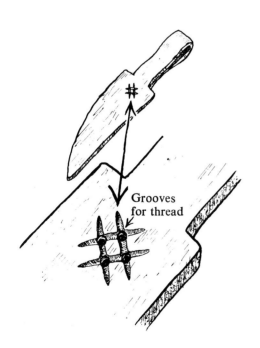

Grooves for thread

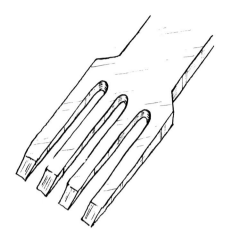

Thonging chisel

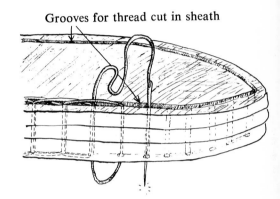

Grooves for thread cut in sheath

will not cut the stitches. Cut little troughs about ¹/₁₆-inch deep where the threads will be. Carefully use a leather knife, or buy a little gouging tool in a leather shop. Now, in the same manner, sew the snap strap to the belt loop.

Next, glue the front piece to the spacer and the spacer to the blade case. Carefully fit the glued pieces together. Check the fit and hammer them together.

Sew quadruple stitches in the upper corners of the blade case. To do this, punch two small holes in line with the other stitching using the smallest blade on a revolving punch. Now, punch holes neatly around the blade case for the stitching. Use a thonging chisel to do this. With a small leather or linoleum gouge, cut a shallow trough along the stitching holes, both front and back, so the stitches will lie flush with the surface of the leather. Sew the blade case with a needle and strong nylon thread. Use a "stair-step" stitch, which is very strong and beautiful. With this stitch, the thread goes two holes forward on the top side, then one hole back, two forward, one back, et cetera.

Set the snaps on the snap strap. The strap that folds on the bottom should have the female snap, and the one on top should have the male. Make the snap fit snugly around the knife handle. Leave a little tab on the end of the strap. Cover the inside surface of the female snap with a very thin circle of leather so it won't abrade against the handle. Hold this pad in place with epoxy cement.

Finally, bevel the sides of the blade case with the belt sander and dye any areas of the sheath that need it.

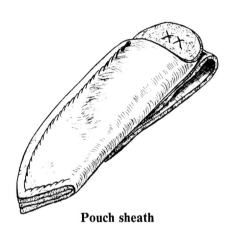

Pouch sheath

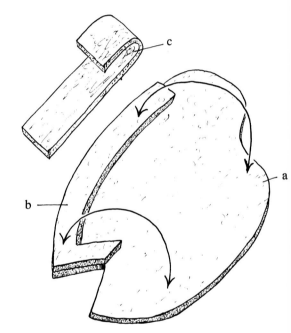

Making a Pouch Sheath

Many of the techniques are the same for this sheath. It, too, is made of 7- to 8-ounce oak- or French-tanned leather. But for this sheath you will soak the leather in water so that it can be molded to the knife. When it dries, the leather will be very stiff and will retain the molded shape.

Wrap the knife in masking tape or aluminum foil so it will be kept dry. Lay out the leather. Place the knife on the leather and draw a line about ¾ inch wider than the outside of the knife. Then, carefully roll the knife over on the handle so it is lying on its other side and trace ¾ inch wider than this silhouette. Draw the top of the sheath lower in the front than in the back. Cut out the piece using a sharp razor-knife.

Soak piece (**a**) for about fifteen minutes in a pan of water. When the leather is completely pliable, begin to mold the leather tightly around the knife. When the leather conforms tightly to the knife, set the leather-wrapped knife in a warm place to dry. If you are in a real hurry, you can place it directly under a warm light bulb, turning it every ten minutes or so. Be very careful if you are using French leather since it can easily become too brittle when exposed to heat.

While the main piece is drying, draw and cut out the belt loop. Again, make this piece proportional to the size of the knife and the sheath. It would usually be between 2½ and 4 inches long. Bevel the edges and corners of the leather. Punch the holes, and cut the small troughs to inset the stitches.

Now that the body of the sheath is dry, match up the holes with the ones on the belt loop and punch and inset them. Double-check the area around the top of the sheath. Make sure that there is enough clearance for the fingers to comfortably grasp the end of the handle. Trace and cut out the blade spacer B. The thickness of the spacer will determine how tightly the sheath will grip the knife, so trim it until the knife feels nice and snug when you hold it together in your hand.

Dye all parts of the leather that will not be glued. Glue and sew on the belt loop using inset stitches. Glue and sew the blade case together, starting with quadruple stitches at the top. Bevel the edges of the sheath and touch up with dye.

This whole process will become clearer when you look at the photos that accompany the instructions for making a snap pouch, or snouch, sheath. As with many other things in life, you may have to try it a few times before you're any good at it.

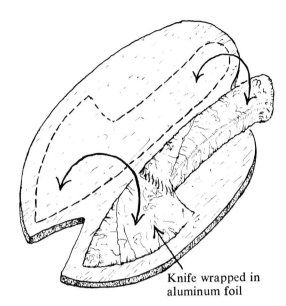

Knife wrapped in aluminum foil

Measuring the sheath

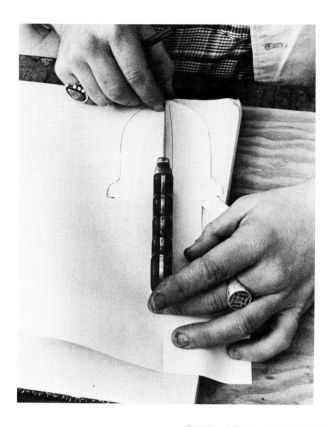

1. Draw out the pattern on a piece of paper. The knife should be able to "roll" from one side to another and stay in position on each side of the pattern.

2. Soak the leather in a dish of water.

3. Lay out the knife in preparation for the molding operation.

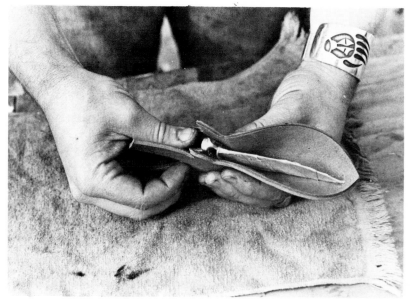

4. Squeeze the leather around the bolster-finger guard. The blade is covered with masking tape and Vaseline. The Vaseline keeps the saw-blade steel from rusting during the drying step.

5. Press the blade case nice and flat.

6. Complete the molding so that the snap strap fits nicely around the finger guard. It should be placed in a warm spot to dry.

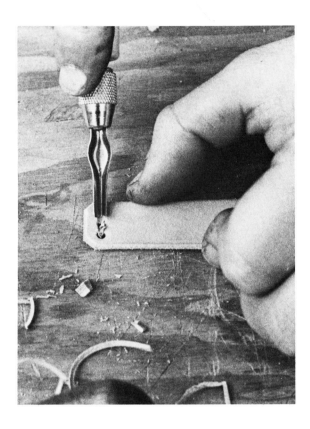

7. Use a gouge to inset the stitches in the belt loop.

8. Shave the spacer to the proper thickness to hold the knife snugly in the case.

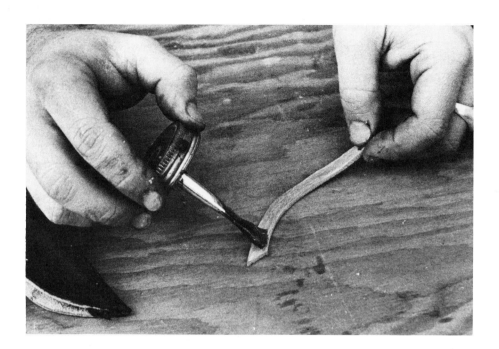

9. Coat each surface with cobbler's cement for a proper bond.

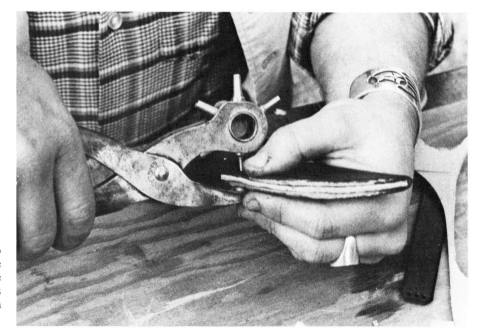

10. Punch two larger holes at the top of the blade case so there is room to begin with a quadruple stitch.

11. Use a thonging chisel to punch out the stitching holes around the blade case.

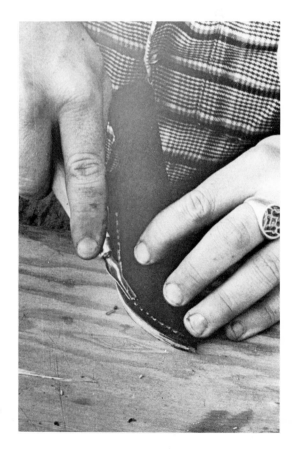

12. Gouge out the shallow trough to inset the stitches.

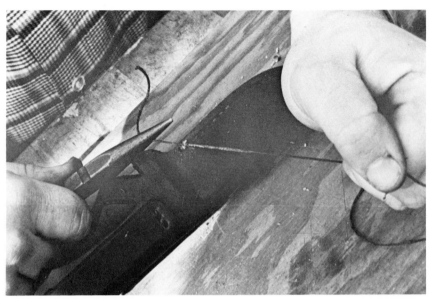

13. After the thread has been wrapped around four times on the top stitch, it is tied tightly with a square knot. The knot is then deftly pulled around so that it is hidden inside the stitching hole. The blade case is then hand-sewn with a stair-step stitch as shown above.

14. The edges of the blade case are beveled in two different ways. The belt sander actually does a nicer job because it polishes and burnishes the leather if you use an old belt.

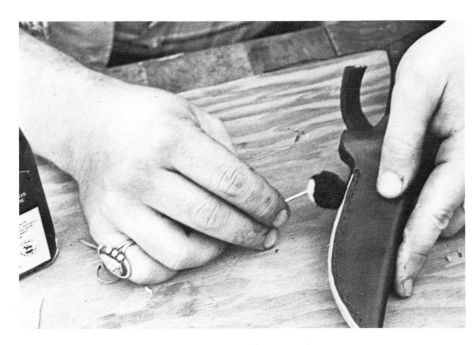

15. Black dye around the blade case and on all the edges adds a subtle touch of elegance to the sheath. You can also buff the sheath very lightly on a clean wheel with no compound. This will impart a soft luster to the leather. There are a number of sealers and finishers on the market that you can try.

16. Use the horn of the anvil to set the snap. An additional step, not shown, is to cover the inside metal surface of the snap with thin leather so that it will not scrape the knife handle. This leather pad is held in place with epoxy cement.

Appendix

Introduction to Alloy Steels

The concepts presented so far are age-old, and the techniques probably haven't changed drastically in the past fifty years. Nevertheless, it is possible now to make a better blade than would have been feasible only twenty-five years ago. This is because metallurgy has developed new alloys and techniques for heat-treatment that allow us to take fuller advantage of the tremendous potential of steel. We now have greater freedom and more precise control in terms of what we can do with tool steel.

The disadvantage to this, of course, is that instead of things being nice and simple, with only one basic kind of steel and only one basic kind of heat-treatment, there are now literally hundreds of kinds of steel, each with special attributes and problems and its own peculiar treatment requirements.

The purpose of this appendix is to help you understand alloy steel better and to give you the technical information you need to take advantage of the super-steels. We will talk theoretically about the function of alloys in steel and then we will look at a few steels that are popular among knifemakers. Hopefully, when we are done, you can put this information together with what we covered in the first twenty chapters and make the knife of your dreams.

A one-chapter summary on metallurgy and the use of tool steels will not provide you with *all* you need to know. This is a very broad and technical field, and a thorough treatment of the topic would take most of us half a lifetime. However, if you are new to tool steels, I am sure you will find the following information quite helpful.

As we said way back in chapter 1, alloy steels are all made to do something that plain carbon steel won't do. By the careful addition of certain *alloying elements,* the following advantages can be realized in tool steel:

1. Increased working temperature, where steel can be brought up to as high as 1,100°F. without losing its hardness.

2. Increased wear resistance at the same hardness.
3. Increased toughness and strength at the same hardness.
4. Less distortion exhibited, or controlled distortion during the hardening process.
5. Increased resistance to corrosion.

Some of these qualities are advantageous to the knifemaker and some are irrelevant. Increased toughness, wear resistance, and resistance to corrosion are definite advantages to a good blade, while the ability to work under tremendous heat probably won't be germane to you. Control over warpage distortion is important to the knifemaker, but control over size distortion is of dubious value; a change in size of a few thousands of an inch is quite irrelevant.

When we talk about alloy steels, these five sought-after qualities keep cropping up because they are integral to the science of metallurgy. Just keep in mind the particular qualities that you, as a steel user, are looking for in a steel.

Keep in mind that this chapter is not only an *introduction* to exotic steels, but it should also serve as a reference as questions about your experimentation may arise. A fact that may seem trivial, or irrelevant, may later serve as a hinge upon which your entire conceptual framework rotates.

In addition, as you read other, more technical books on steel, and perhaps talk to metallurgists, you will have this relatively simple introduction as a basis.

The Anatomy and Physiology of Alloy Steel

Steel is a combination of iron and carbon. In the simplest condition, the softened state, carbon is in chemical combination with a small percentage of iron, in the form of iron carbide, called *carbide* or *cementite*. The remainder of iron, the vast matrix in which the molecules of cementite are held suspended, is composed of simple iron molecules, or *ferrite*.

When the steel is heated, the molecules of ferrite and the molecules of cementite react to form grains of *austenite* that grow larger until they impinge upon one another. Further heating produces larger and larger grains of austenite and a solution of excess carbide. This point is called "reaching solution."

Grain size and steel strength are inversely proportional. Steel with large grain size is inherently weaker because of the diminished contact between the grains, and because the bonds between the grains become weaker as grain size increases.

When the steel is properly quenched after reaching solution, the austenite forms into a hard, needle-like structure called martensite. The free carbides "freeze" (become solid) and remain as hard stones in a less hard, but rigid matrix of martensitic formation.

The tempering process reduces some of the stress caused by the martensitic transformation, leaving a hard, tough matrix supporting very hard carbide particles. The hardness and toughness of the matrix, and the hardness and quantity of the carbides are the stuff of alloy metallurgy.

Adding Alloys

Let's discuss some of the different alloys which are added to this basic system, and what they can do for the effectiveness of steel.

Carbon

As you already know, carbon, the most basic alloy, is used to make the steel harder and more wear-resistant. With plain carbon tool steel, the higher the carbon content, the harder the steel will be when properly quenched, up to about .65 percent carbon, when the steel will become file-hard. Adding more carbon adds to the wear resistance, but not to the hardness. Most carbon tool steel runs around 1 percent carbon, and some runs as high as 1.5 percent carbon. The higher amount of carbon produces very hard and wear-resistant steel, which is tricky to heat-treat and lacks toughness. A high carbon steel's wear resistance is primarily due to the presence of excess carbides. These hard particles act like hard stones embedded in a matrix of resin—the hardness (resistance to indentation) of the material is primarily due to the property of the matrix, but the resistance to abrasion is due to the hardness and number of the stones (or carbide particles). If the steel is heated, causing the martensitic matrix to become weak, wear resistance goes down. Although the free carbides retain their hardness, the iron matrix cannot support them, and they are pushed aside by abrasion, like stones in mud.

Manganese

One limitation in plain carbon steel is the fast, critical, quenching speed. This means that while small workpieces may be cooled quickly enough to properly harden, massive pieces will not cool quickly enough in the center, producing a hard surface only and a soft center. The principal effect of adding manganese as an alloy is to decrease the critical quenching speed, thus dramatically increasing the hardness penetration.

Carbon steel with manganese can undergo "oil hardening," instead of "water hardening." This steel tends to be more stable in the quench and less likely to crack, because the shock of quenching is less traumatic in oil than in water.

Chromium

Like manganese, chromium also increases hardness penetration. When 5.0 percent chromium is added along with 1.0 percent manganese, the critical quenching speed is further reduced, forming the basis for a very important class of "air hardening" tool steels.

A second advantage to adding chromium is that it combines with the free carbides, making them even harder, and giving the steel increased wear resistance. The toughness of the steel is increased also. When about 11 percent to 14 percent chromium is added to high-carbon tool steel, the wear resistance is increased remarkably, and this is a most important factor for the knifemaker.

Chromium imparts the very important factor of corrosion resistance. While no tool steel is completely "stainless", the more chrome present in the analysis, the nearer to this goal the steel becomes. At low percentages, say around 5 percent, the resistance is noticeable. At 11 percent, the resistance to rust and darkening is marked, and at 14 percent and above the steel is often referred to as stainless, though it may still stain and corrode under certain conditions.

High-speed steel has some chrome, which helps maintain the "hot hardness."

Chromium tends to raise somewhat the critical temperature of steel.

Tungsten

Tungsten, added in small amounts, increases wear resistance. At higher percentages, say 4 percent, wear resistance is increased dramatically, as is the ability to retain hardness when heated (hot hardness). Perhaps you have had the experience of trying to grind a tungsten mechanical hacksaw blade, thinking you were going to make a knife out of it. I suspect a few potential knifemakers switched professions after trying to make their first knife out of such a steel. It is difficult to anneal, it won't grind or drill, and you can't cut it with an acetylene torch.

When added in greater quantities, say 15 to 20 percent, in conjunction with about 4 percent chromium, tungsten imparts the quality of "red hardness" to the steel, which means that the steel will not become annealed and lose its working hardness even if it is heated to a dull red temperature, 1,100°F.

Red hardness allows tools to be used to cut very hard materials at very high speeds and for prolonged periods, thus the name "high-speed steel."

Tungsten, like chromium, combines with the free carbides, producing extreme wear resistance without undue loss of toughness.

Molybdenum

Like chromium, molybdenum increases hardness penetration and inclines the steel towards slower quenching mediums. Molybdenum is also used in place of, or in conjunction with, tungsten and chromium to produce high-speed tool steels. Molybdenum imparts toughness and hardness to the matrix, hardens the carbides, and gives the steel hot hardness.

Silicon

Small amounts are added to aid in the manufacture of steel. When added in concert with other alloys, silicon increases toughness, strength, and hardness penetration.

Nickel

Nickel adds to wear resistance and toughness when used together with other alloys. It slows the critical quenching speed.

Vanadium

This element helps steel withstand high heat, either during high temperature hardening by controlling grain growth, or in conjunction with tungsten, chromium, and other alloys in high-speed and hot-working die steels.

Phosphorus and Sulfur

Regarded as harmful impurities, phosphorus and sulfur are kept to a minimum. The exception is their use in improving the machinability of some high-alloy tool steels.

There are other alloys used in steel manufacture, of course, but these are the ones we are concerned with in knifemaking steels.

Popular Knifemaking Steels

Let's take a look at some of the steels now in use by the top knifemakers. These steels vary greatly, as do the knifemakers who use them. There are

AISI	C	Mn	Ph	S	Si	Cr	Mo	Ni	W
W2	.6–1.4	.25			.25				
O1	1.0	1.35			.35	.50			.50
L6	.7–.9	.35–.55	.025	.01	.25	.03		1.4–2.6	
A2	1.0	.6			.25–.40	5.0	1.0		
F2	1.3	.25			.25	.3 OR .3			3.5
M2	.85	.25			.30	4.2	5.0		6.35
D2	1.5	25/40			30/50	11.5	1.0		
440C	1.0	.5			.40	17.0	.45	.20	
154CM	1.05	.6	.03	.03	.25	14.0	4.0		

many considerations in choosing a grade of steel. These include all the particular criteria for a good blade, such as hardness, wear resistance, corrosion resistance, and toughness, but also cost and availability, and the difficulty, time, and technical problems involved in heat-treatment. So, with these factors in mind, let's see what kind of options we have.

This is a chart of the vital statistics of nine tool steels commonly used by knifemakers. Look through the chart, then refer back to it for comparisons among the steels when we discuss each one individually.

The steels have been arranged roughly in order of their variance from plain carbon steel in terms of alloy content, performance, and hardening technology.

V	Quench Temp.	** Quench	Hardness at Quench	Wear Resistance	Toughness	Grain Size
.25	1,400–1,550		65–67	2–4	3–7	9
	1,450–1,500	O	61–64	4	3	8.5
.15	1,475–1,550	O	58–63	2–3	4–6	8
.20	1,700–1,800	A	63–65	6	4	8.5
.25	1,450–1,600	W	65–68	8	2–6	10
1.9	2,175–2,250	O A B	64–66	7	3	9.5
.90	1,775–1,850	A	61–64	8	2	7.5
	1,850–1,900	A	59	NO DATA	NO DATA	NO DATA
	2,000	A	63	NO DATA *	NO DATA *	NO DATA *

The above data summarized from *Tool Steels,* by G. A. Roberts, J. C. Hamaker, Jr., and A. R. Johnson, first published in 1962 by the American Society for Metals, Metals Park, Ohio, and information presented in manufacturers' specification sheets.

*I haven't been able to find specific performance data but from the analysis and reports from users, wear resistance should be equivalent to D2, but with greater toughness.

**O-oil   W-water
A-air   B-brine

Take a cursory look at the above chart. What are some of the basic trends among the steels? The basic tendency, which is predictable from our above discussion, is that as carbon content goes up, hardness and wear resistance go up also, but toughness goes down. Any individual steel, if it is tempered hard, will be less tough but more wear-resistant. The American Iron and Steel Institute organizes the hundreds of different steels in type categories, based either upon their hardening method, the use the steel was designed for, or their metallurgical analysis.

W—Water hardening
S—Shock resisting
F—Carbon-tungsten
L—Low alloy
O—Oil hardening
D—Die steels
A—Air hardening
T—Tungsten alloys
M—Molybdenum alloys

The numbers behind the letters are designations for different particular grades within a general steel type. For example, W2 is the second water-hardening steel listed. These grades differ from one another in type and amount of alloys used. Variation occurs among steels of the same type and grade, due to special purpose design and different manufacturing techniques.

W2

This steel is designated as carbon-vanadium steel because of the small amount of vanadium, which adds some tendency to inhibit grain growth if the steel is overheated during hardening. However, this quality is not marked due to the small amount of vanadium present, and for all practical purposes should be regarded as plain, water-hardening carbon steel.

W2 is available in a range of carbon contents from .60 percent to 1.4 percent. Look over to the "performance" columns and see that this gives you a wear resistance factor of from 2 to 4 and a toughness of from 3 to 7. We run into the series of trade-offs. I would surmise that a carbon content of about .90 percent to 1.00 percent would give your best all-around balance between hardness and toughness for knife blades, depending upon the intended use, blade thickness, and so on.

To harden W2, heat the steel evenly to the critical point, say 1,500°F. and quench in water or brine. This radical quench is necessary for W2, but it is a distinct disadvantage because rapid cooling leads to possible warpage and cracking, especially if the shape of your knife is complex. For example, if the blade has a thick back and a thin edge, or a brazed bolster, the cooling speeds of different parts of the knife will vary with the different mass areas, causing the blade to crack where a thin part comes up to a massive part. This steel could be described as risky.

Aside from a slightly higher initial hardness due to the water quench, the hardness curve for W2 is about the same as that for L6 saw-blade steel, but one or two points higher across the board for the higher percentages of carbon.

The backbone and handle area can be annealed in the manner described on pages 117–19.

W2 (1%)
Rockwell
Hardness

65	64	63	61	59	57	55
300	350	400	450	500	550	600

Degrees F.

The main advantage of W2 is its low cost and the choice of carbon contents.

01

Classed as a cold-work die steel, this grade is most useful for a wide variety of tool applications. The manganese content allows this steel to be oil quenched. Thus the steel is more stable, since it is less likely to warp or crack in the hardening process. The .50 percent chromium and .50 percent tungsten aid in the resistance to grain growth.

Heat-treating instructions are similar to those given in chapter 7 for L6 saw-blade steel.

Note that the slightly higher wear resistance and the slightly lower toughness factors for 01, when compared with L6, directly reflects its slightly higher carbon content.

01 (1%)
**Rockwell
Hardness**

62	61	59	58	56	55	54
300	350	400	450	500	550	600

Degrees F.

L6

If you have used, or plan to use, saw-blade steel for knifemaking, there is a good chance it is L6 steel or something similar. The L stands for low alloy, indicating that this steel is largely plain carbon steel, but with some refined characteristics. It is considered a nickel-based steel. Nickel enters the ferride matrix of the steel, giving it greater toughness. The wear resistance of this steel is about the same as plain carbon steel of equal carbon content, but the steel is far tougher, approaching the toughness of silicon shock-resisting steels.

This steel is used in woodcutting saws, knives, shear blades, et cetera—tools that require good wear resistance and great toughness.

Heat-treatment is given in detail in chapter 7, but here are the Rockwell numbers for different tempering temperatures.

L6
**Rockwell
Hardness**

63	62	61	60	58	57	56	55
300	350	400	450	500	550	600	650

Degrees F.

A2

This is a higher alloy and a better grade of knife steel than any discussed so far. It has increased wear resistance and increased toughness over 01. In addition, A2 has mild corrosion resistance due to the 5 percent chromium in the analysis. However, as you might guess, this steel is somewhat expensive when compared to the simpler steels, and the heat-treatment requirements are much more elaborate. The hardening temperature is 1,750 to 1,800°F. Not only that, but there are two other complexities: stress-relieving and atmosphere.

Before bringing the steel up to the hardening temperature, it should be heated slowly and soaked at 1,400°F. for fifteen minutes or so to relieve stresses caused by grinding the steel, and then brought up to the hardening temperature. Normally, this double heating requires two kilns, because the knife cannot stay at high temperature for forty-five minutes while the kiln slowly heats up from 1,400° to 1,800°F. This would cause unnecessary grain growth as well as possible excess decarburization, and would be an inefficient use of kiln space and fuel.

The second problem is atmosphere. When most alloy steels are heated to above 1,200°F. or so, the problems of scale formation and decarburization appear. These problems become pronounced when the steel reaches the high-hardening temperatures of 1,700°F. and more. There are two generally recognized solutions to this problem: (1) controlling the type of atmosphere inside the kiln, and (2) packing the workpiece in a small container with a material such as cast-iron filings or spent coke.

Most knifemakers send steels such as A2 to professionals for heat-treatment. There are a number of shops that do nothing but harden and temper tools. They have the equipment to fully harden and temper A2 or other steel without causing the least bit of scale, decarburization, or even discoloration. The heat-treating shop can also guarantee your knife will be exactly as hard as you request it. The professional heat-treatment shop takes all the guesswork and some of the fun out of the heat-treatment process.

I am presently experimenting with simple methods to overcome these problems for the knifemaker, but at this point I can't be of much help to you. So, for A2 steel I recommend that you send your knife blades to a hardening shop. It is more economical and will cost you far less if you can send in a number of blades of the same analysis in one batch.

But if you are as stubborn as I am, you'll want to temper them yourself. So do it this way. After preheating, bring the steel to the critical temperature for a few minutes, then bring it out to cool in still air. Tempering begins when the piece is just cool enough to hold in your bare hands.

Here are the tempering temperatures and the hardnesses they produce with A2. It is recommended that you temper twice for additional toughness without a sacrifice in hardness.

			A2 Rockwell Hardness			
63	62.5	62	61	60	58	58
300	350	400	450	500	550	600
			Degrees F.			

The recommended hardness for A2 steel is Rc62.

There is an additional touch which can be added to this standard process, which may give you a little added hardness and wear resistance with no reduction in toughness in this steel. It is called a sub-zero quench. If the steel, after reaching room temperature, is brought down to about -100° to -120°F. a net gain of two to three points on the Rockwell scale can be gained, without any sacrifice in toughness. This happens because at room temperature not all the austenite has transformed into martensite. It takes the additional sub-zero quench to fully utilize the potential of this material. This sub-zero quench must be done prior to the tempering treatment, however, or the retained austenite will be stabilized and unresponsive to a subsequent refrigeration quench.

If you want to try this treatment in your workshop, you can achieve a decent sub-zero treatment using dry ice, which will take the blade down to about -109°F.

Let's suppose you went ahead against my recommendation and heat-treated the blade yourself. Let's hope you made the blade slightly thicker than you want it so you can grind off the scale and the soft, decarburized skin, and complete the polishing process without making the blade too thin. Use a simple scratch test with a blade of known hardness. A hard blade will scratch the soft, decarburized skin but not the hardened steel underneath.

If you had a brazed bolster on the blade, you observed that the brass melted into a small puddle at the bottom of the kiln. If so, throw the blade away. Next time plan on *soldering* on a bolster *after* the heat-treatment and final polishing steps are completed.

Also, with A2, don't try to anneal the backbone and handle areas after tempering. This will cause stresses in the blade and won't really improve the knife. Instead, drill the holes for the rivets and/or pins prior to the hardening step.

F2

F2 is classified as a tungsten finishing steel. It is designed for jobs that require a very hard, wear-resistant cutting edge and good toughness. The water quench produces some distortion. The extreme wear resistance accrues from the high carbon content and the hard iron, tungsten, and chromium carbides held in suspension by the very hard matrix of martensite.

It is important not to heat F2 over the 1,600°F. temperature or marked grain growth and decarburization will result. Therefore, as with A2, a preheating step may be wise to insure the complete austenizing without undue structural deterioration. F2 becomes very hard, with a Rockwell of 66 to 70 after quenching, depending upon the initial hardening temperature of between 1,450° and 1,600°F.

Here are the hardness levels as a function of the tempering temperatures for F2.

F2
Rockwell
Hardness

67	65	64	63	62.5	61	59
300	350	400	450	500	550	600

Degrees F.

Generally, this steel is not tempered above 375°F., because the compressive strength goes down as the hardness goes down, above 300°F.

A sub-zero quench is not used with this alloy.

As with A2, do not try to anneal the backbone and handle area but instead predrill the handle area prior to hardening.

Unless you have time to experiment with the different variables, I recommend that you have this grade, as well as the ones to follow, professionally heat-treated. If you decide to do your own treating, you should have each knife professionally tested for hardness until you feel sure about what you are doing.

M2

This is a high-speed steel designed for use in the form of cutting tools. The steel can retain a Rockwell hardness of 55 at temperatures of over

1,000°F. Originally, the high-speed steels were made with about 18 percent tungsten, with smaller amounts of chrome and vanadium. However, during World War II tungsten was in short supply, and molybdenum was used as a partial substitute. It worked so well that today molybdenum is quite a common ingredient in steels that require hot hardness, high "harden-ability" and wear resistance.

In this analysis, the molybdenum, tungsten, and chrome strengthen the iron matrix as well as augmenting the free carbide microstructures. The grade shows a good wear resistance, only fair toughness, but unfortunately is difficult to heat-treat due to high hardening temperatures.

If you are daring enough to try heat-treating M2 at home, be sure you leave plenty of steel to grind off because of the deep decarburization that will result from a lack of controlled atmosphere in your furnace. I suggest an air quench.

After hardening, this steel is very stressed, brittle, and dimensionally unstable. Tempering reduces this "wild" state, and can be done at about 1,100°F. for one hour. During this process, M2 drops about five points in hardness, then regains its losses, ending up at the same or higher hardness than it had achieved at quench. M2 is often tempered in the above manner a second time to produce the hardnesses below.

M2
Rockwell
Hardness

65	63	61	62	66	60
200	400	600	800	1,000	1,200

Degrees F.

Again let me suggest seeing your local heat-treatment professional.

D2

Now here is a steel that a lot of knifemakers have used. It was developed around World War I, so it has been around a long time. It is not a real hard steel. It derives its exceptional wear resistance from the combination of high carbon and chrome, which produces hard chromium carbides.

In addition, D2 is somewhat stain-resistant. The high chromium content maintains a very bright finish in the face of many corrosives, such as citrus and other acidic foods.

A disadvantage is that this steel is somewhat brittle. Although much has been made of its brittleness, part of the design of the knife is the steel. If you want to use your knife as a pry bar or as a throwing knife, then D2 wouldn't be the obvious choice. On the other hand, if you want a steel that holds an excellent edge, is stain-resistant, and isn't too difficult to heat-treat, then D2 might be a good choice for you.

As with the other high-alloy steels, do the drilling prior to hardening.

It is advisable to preheat the steel slowly to about 1,400°F. before bringing it up to the hardening temperature of 1,800°F. Again, when a controlled-atmosphere furnace is not available, it is advisable to pack the blade in paper, then in a container with an inert material such as dry cast-iron chips or spent pitch coke.

A less acceptable alternative is to harden the blade prior to the 240-grit abrasive step and then regrind the blade with this belt, removing the decarburized or overcarburized skin that will be about .002 or .003 inch thick.

Begin tempering as soon as the blade is cool enough to handle with bare hands. Tempering time is three to five hours.

		D2 **Rockwell** **Hardness**		
62–64	60–62	59–61	58–60	57–59
300	400	500 **Degrees F.**	600	700

I recommend a double tempering of 400°F., producing a Rockwell of 60–62.

440C

Here we are approaching the ideal of corrosion resistance, but unfortunately we have to sacrifice a little on some other important points. As you can see, the hardness at quench is a not-too-hard 59, and any tempering to reduce brittleness will reduce hardness even further. Therefore, the tradeoffs with this type of steel are somewhat severe. You can have a fairly soft blade that is fairly tough, or a fairly tough blade that is fairly soft. The remaining alternatives are to have a blade that is either too soft, and thus also not wear-resistant enough, or too brittle, and no one wants that. This grade of steel thus is not highly respected among professional knifemakers. It is, however, heavily used among the makers of production knives, from kitchen knives to hunting knives and folders. It is also a popular choice among makers of fine collector's knives, which are made for appearance, not use.

The 440C is a good steel if your main concern is corrosion resistance. Let's face it, the primary function of many knives is to be beautiful, or to perform around salt water or spray, or in the tropics, and for those knives, 440C is a wise choice.

Heat-treat 440C like you would D2, except bring the steel up a little hotter in the hardening step.

Here are the hardness values for tempering.

440C
Rockwell
Hardness

59	59	56	54
AQ	212	400	600

Degrees F.

I recommend about a 350° draw, which will give you a hardness in the 57–58 range, with good toughness.

154CM

By replacing four percentage points of chromium with molybdenum, 440C was modified to produce an increase in hardenability of four points on the Rockwell scale, and maybe a point or two over that by using a sub-zero quench. There is no sacrifice in toughness. Incidental to the knifemaker, this steel was designed as a hot-work stainless.

The steel lacks performance data because it is relatively new and is classified as a stainless, rather than a tool steel. However, the manufacturers claim, and users agree, that this steel performs like a top-quality hot-work steel. This would place it roughly in the category of M2 and F2 in terms of performance, but with the additional important quality of stain and corrosion resistance.

Of the steels that I know are within the realm, pricewise, I would choose 154CM as the best all-round knife steel for the higher-quality user and collector's knives.

One disadvantage that I have encountered is a lack of choice as far as stock sizes. For example, my supplier will only take orders for one gauge, approximately ⅜ inch, which is fine for some knives, but a little thick for kitchen knives.

Heat-treatment for 154CM is similar in spirit to that of other high-alloy hot-work steels.

After preheating to 1,550°F., the steel can be hardened by oil or air quenching at 2,000°F. Leave the steel at the hardening temperature for about twenty minutes to complete the information of austenite.

After quenching, refrigerate to -100°F. for one hour. Temper twice at the level of your choice, according to the following table:

		154CM Rockwell Hardness		
61	57	61	62	58
As quenched	700	900	1,000	1,050
		Degrees F.		

On Working with the Different Alloys

Here are some comments regarding the different properties of the steels, and some general rules-of-thumb in working with them. Preface each of these statements with the hedge, "in general" or "in most cases," so that we understand that steels are like people: the more complex they are, the more tricky and unpredictable they are to work with. Until you get to know them, that is.

Never cut out a high-alloy steel with a cutting torch. High alloy is anything that requires a hardening temperature of over 1,550°F., that takes more than an hour to temper, or that is air cooled. The cutting torch would set up too many stresses within the steel. It is much better to anneal the steel, according to the proper annealing instructions for that steel, and then use a band saw. If you don't have a band saw, use a thin cutoff wheel or a hacksaw to rough it out, then refine the lines with the grindstone.

Always slowly preheat a high-alloy steel prior to placing in a kiln heated to the hardening temperature. This gently removes the stresses built up within the steel from the initial grinding, so you don't have a sudden, uneven surge of tension release.

Obviously, with the alloys that harden at temperatures above the melting point of brass, you can't very well use a bolster that is brazed on prior to hardening, can you? Therefore, if you want brass or nickel silver pieces incorporated into the handle, you are going to have to solder them after tempering, with low-temperature silver solder.

Index

A Abrasive belts, 30
Abrasive strip drum sanders, 32
Acetylene torch. *See* Torches
Acid, mixing of, for acid etching
  bath, 215–16
Acid bath, agitation in, 222
  for etching blades, 214–24
  light and, 221
  temperature of, 221
Agitation, in acid bath etching,
  222
Air, as quenching bath, 113, 114
Alloy steel, 14
  advantages of, 249, 250
  characteristics of, 250, 251
  working with, 265, 266
Alloys, addition of, to steel, 251–
  54. *See also name of alloy*
Amperage, of electric power, 23,
  24
Animals, as source of handle material, 152, 153
Annealing, of backbone, 117–20
  bolster and, 119
  definition of, 105
  handle and, 117–20
Antlers, as handles, 152, 153
  method for making, 177–80
Anvils, 36
Arbor, grinding, 26, 27
Artwork, for blade designs, 212,
  213, 225, 226
  samples of, 225–31
Austenite, definition of, 109
Austenizing, critical range and,
  109

B Backbone, annealing of, 117–20
Band saws, 34
  for cutting steel, 64, 65
Band saw blades, as knife blades,
  15
Bath, acid, for etching blades,
  214–24
  quenching, steel hardening
    and, 113–15
Belt grinders, 28–33

belts for, 28–30
oil-cooled, 209
parts of, 25–28
water-cooled, 207–9
work wheels for, 30, 31
Belt sanders, 28–33
  for handle shaping, 168–70
  platens for, 30, 31
  water-cooled three-wheel,
    207
  work wheels for, 30, 31
Belts, abrasive, 30
  for grinders, 28–30
  grit sizes for, 171, 172
  for sanders, 28–30
Beveling, of sheaths, 235
Bevels, 69, 70
  rolled edge, 73, 74
Biting, in acid bath etching, 223,
  224
Bits, countersink, method for
  making, 146, 147
  drill, 138, 139
    sharpening of, 139, 140
Blades. *See also* Steel
  back of, finishing of, 172
  carbon steel, hardening of,
    105–20
    heat-treatment of, 105–20
  cutting out, 61–68
  discoloration of, 106–8
  dropped, finger guard for, 74,
    75
  grinding of, 2–4, 69–78
  hammering of, 123, 124
  heat-treating of, 76
  polishing of, 129–34
  preparation of, for etching,
    211–13
  problems of, remedies for,
    123–26
  qualities of, 11–13
  regrinding of, 129–34
  saw blades as, 1, 14–16
  shape of, refinement of,
    65–67
  steel for, 14–16
  straightening of, 67, 123–26
  tempering of, 116, 117
  twisted, remedy for, 124
  warpage of, 106, 107

Bolster, annealing and, 119
  brazing of, 81, 82, 86–91
  connection of, with pins, 102,
    103
  construction of, 79–103
  fairing down, 91
  finishing of, 172
  fitting scales to, 160, 161
  for partial-tang handle, 97–99
  ready-made, 101, 102
  silver-soldering of, to butt
    cup, 100–102
  straightening of, 125, 126
Bone handles, 152, 153
Boning knives, 47
Brake-shoe rivets, 145–49
Brass, hole in, removal of, 96
  selection of, 81, 82
Brass pins, method for making,
  143–45
Brazing, of bolster, 81, 82, 86–91
  of butt piece, 91
Bread knives, 49, 50
Brine, as quenching bath, 113,
  115
Buffer, for stropping edges, 191,
  192
Buffing, of knives, 183–86
  safety factors in, 183–86
Buffing wheels, 183
  cleaning of, 186
Burins, etching, 212
Burr, formation of, 189–91
Butcher knives, 45
Butt cap, silver-soldering of, to
  bolster, 100–102
Butt piece, brazing of, 91
Butt plate, construction of, 79–103

C Carbon, as steel alloy, 251
Carbon steel, 14
Carbon steel blade, hardening of,
  105–20
    heat-treatment of, 105–20
Carving forks, 46, 47
Carving knives, 46
Cast iron, description of, 109
Chef's knife, 42, 43
  bevel on, 73
Chisel, thonging, 237
Chopping knives, 2, 47–49

Chromium, as steel alloy, 252
Circular saw blades, as knife
    blades, 15
Clearance, for sanders, 29, 30
Cleavers, meat, 51, 52
Color, of steel, quenching
    temperature and, 112, 113
        tempering and, 116, 117
Concave bevel, 70
Convex bevel, 69, 70, 73, 74
Corrosion, of saw-blade steel, 17
Corrosion resistance, blade
    quality and, 12, 13
Countersink bits, method for mak-
    ing, 146, 147
Cracks, hairline, in handle, 174
Critical range, austenizing and,
    109
Critical temperature, of steel, 109
Cutting, of slabs, 157
        of steel, with band saw, 64, 65
        with torch, 63, 64

D Danish oil, for handles, 175
Decarburization, of steel, 106, 108
Decay, internal, of steel, 106, 108
Design, on blade, etching of,
    211–32
        of knives, 7
Discoloration, of steel, 106–8
Drag saws, as knife blades, 15
Drawing, on steel, 61, 62
Drill bits, 138, 139
        sharpening of, 139, 140
Drill presses, 33
Drilling, of rivet holes, 137–40
        of slab holes, 161, 162
Dropped blade, finger guard for,
    74, 75
Dropped-edge knives, 55
Drum sanders, abrasive strip, 32
    sleeve-type, 31, 32
Drying kiln, 154, 155

E Edges, on blades, 69–74. *See also*
    Bevels
        grinding of, 69–78
        stropping of, 191, 192
        types of, 69–73
        wavy, remedy for, 125
Electric kilns, 34–36

Electric motors, choice of, factors
    in, 21, 22
Electric power, 23–25
Epoxy glue, use of, 163, 164
Etching, acid bath for, 214–24
        agitation in, 222
        of designs, in steel, 211–31
        multilayer, 225
        tool for, 212
Etching burins, 212
"Exotic" steel, 14

F Filet knives, 43–45
Filler, for wood, 174
Finger grips, method for making,
    170, 171
Finger guard, construction of,
    79–103
        for dropped blade, 74, 75
        ready-made, 101, 102
Flap-sanders, 32, 33
Flap-sanding, of handle, 174, 175
Fluid, for quenching. *See*
    Quenching bath
        tooling, use of, 140
Forges, 36
Forks, carving, 46, 47
Four-wheel band saws, 34
French chef's knife, 42, 43
Full-tang handles, 56–58
        bolster for, 82–96
        method for making, 157–75

G Glue, epoxy, use of, 163, 164
Grain growth, quenching
    temperature and, 113
        steel and, 111
Grinder marks, removal of,
    130–34
Grinders, belt. *See* Belt grinders
        high-speed, 25–28
        parts of, 25–28
Grinding, of blades, 2–4, 69–78
        heat-treating and, 75–77
        of knives. *See type of knife;*
            e.g., **Filet knives**
        marks from, removal of,
            130–34
        technique of, 71, 72
        after tempering, 129–34

Grinding arbor, 26, 27
Grinding wheels, 28
        safety factors in, 25, 26
Grips, for fingers, method for
    making, 170, 171
Grits, for grinding belts, 171, 172
Grounding, of electric motors, 25
Guard, finger. *See* Finger guard
Guides, pressure, for grinder, 27,
    28

H Hacksaw blades, as knife blades,
    16
Hairline cracks, in handle,
    remedy for, 174
Half-tang handles, 56, 58
Hammering, of blades, 123, 124
Handles, annealing and, 117–20
        from antlers, method for mak-
            ing, 177–80
        construction of, 4–6
        Danish oil for, 175
        design of, 58
        flap-sanding of, 174, 175
        full-tang, 2
            bolster for, 82–96
            method for making, 157–75
        materials for, 151–53
            drying kiln for, 154, 155
            moisture and, 153, 154
            stability and, 153, 154
        partial-tang, bolster for,
            97–99
            method for making, 177–80
        shaping of, 168–75
        types of, 56–58
        weight reduction in, 138
        wood for, 4
Hand-sharpening, 192–96
Hand-stropping, 196
Hardening, of carbon steel blades,
    105–20
        definition of, 105
        of steel, quenching bath for,
            113–15
            quenching temperature
                for, 111–13
Hardness, blade quality and, 12,
    13
        degree of, 120

spark test for, 119, 120
of steel, 106, 108–11
tempering and, 110
Hatchets, 56
Heat-treating, of carbon steel
blade, 105–20
grinding and, 75–77
preparation for, 76
High-speed grinders, 25–28
Holes, for rivets, method for drilling, 137–40
placement of, 137
in slabs, method for drilling,
161, 162
Hollow grind, 72, 73
Horsepower, definition of, 21

I Individual production, vs. mass,
203, 204
Internal decay, of steel, 106, 108
Internal stress, of steel, 110
Iron, cast, description of, 109
Ivory handles, 152

K Kiln, drying, 154, 155
electric, 34–36
Knifemaker's rivets, 149
Knifemaking, overview of, 9–17
skills in, 11
steel for, 254–66
qualities of, 254–66
step-by-step checklist for,
199–201
strategy for, 205, 206
tools for, 19–38. *See also type
and name of tool*
workmanship in, 7, 8
Knives, biting of, 223, 224
blades for, from saw blades,
1, 14–16. *See also* Blades
buffing of, 183–86
characteristics of, 6–9
collector's, 8, 9
design of, 7, 58
kinds of, 41–56. *See also type
of knife; e.g.,* Vegetable
knives
maintenance of, 197
production of, notes on,
203–9

quality of, materials and, 8
sharpening of, 189–96
steels for, qualities of, 254–66
user's, 8, 9

L Leather, in sheathmaking. *See*
Sheathmaking
Light, in acid bath etching, 221
in workshop, 38

M Maintenance, of knives, 197
Manganese, as steel alloy, 252
Mártensite, definition of, 109
Mass production, vs. individual,
203, 204
Materials, for blades, 14–16
for handles, 151–53
knife quality and, 8
Meat cleavers, 51, 52
Mechanical hacksaw blades, as
knife blades, 16
Micarta, as handle material, 153
Micrometers, 36
use of, 75, 76
Moisture, handle material and,
153, 154
Molybdenum, as steel alloy, 253
Motors, choice of, factors in, 21,
22
electric power for, 23–25
variable speed, 22, 23
Multilayer etching, 225

N Nickel, as steel alloy, 253

O Oil, Danish, for handles, 175
as quenching bath, 113–15
Oil-cooled belt grinder, 209
Oxyacetylene torch. *See* Torches

P Paring knives, 51
Partial-tang handle, bolster for,
97–99
method for making, 177–80
Phase, of electric power, 23
Phosphorus, as steel alloy, 254
Pins. *See also* Rivets
brass, method for making,
143–45

Platens, for belt sanders, 30, 31
Polishing, of blades, 129–34
Pouch sheaths, 233, 234
method for making, 238–47
Power, electric, 23–25
electric motors and, 21, 22
Pressure guide, for grinder, 27, 28
Production, of knives, notes on,
203–9
mass vs. individual, 203, 204

Q Quenching bath, steel hardening
and, 113–15
Quenching temperature, steel
hardening and, 111–13

R Range, critical, austenizing and,
109
Regrinding, after tempering, 206,
207. *See also* Grinding
Resistance, to wear, of steel,
108–11
Rests, work. *See* Work rests
Rivets. *See also* Pins
holes for, method for drilling,
137–40
placement of, 137
inexpensive, 145, 146
knifemaker's, 149
method for removing, 148,
149
method for setting, 147, 148
Rolled edge bevel, 73, 74

S Safety, in buffing, 183–86
Sanders, abrasive strip drum, 32
belt. *See* Belt sanders
belts for, 28–30
clearance for, 29, 30
flap-, 32, 33
sleeve-type drum, 31, 32
Sanding, flap-, of handle, 174, 175
Sandwich knives, 50
Saw blades, as knife blades, 1,
14–16
Saw-blade steel, analysis of, 16
corrosion of, 17
types of, 14–16
Saws, band. *See* Band saws
Scale handles, 56

full-tang, method for making, 157–75
Scales, clamping to shank, 163–68
fastening to shank, 164–68
fitting to bolster, 160, 161
fitting to tang, 157–60
Shank, clamping scales to, 163–68
fastening scales to, 164–68
Shape, of blade, refinement of, 65–67
Shaping, of handle, 168–75
Sharpening, of drill bits, 139, 140
of knives, 189–96
by hand, 192–96
Sharpness, method for "seeing," 192
Sheathmaking, 233–47
Sheaths, pouch, 233, 234
method for making, 238–47
snap, 234
method for making, 235–38
"Side" knives. *See* Utility knives
Silicon, as steel alloy, 253
Silver-soldering, of bolster and butt cup, 100–102
Simple wedge bevel, 70
Skinning knives, 52, 53
Slab handles, 56
full-tang, bolster for, 82–96
Slabs, cutting of, 157
holes in, method for drilling, 161, 162
Sleeve-type drum sanders, 31, 32
Snap sheaths, 234
method for making, 235–38
Spark test, for hardness, 119, 120
Stability, handle material and, 153, 154
Stag handles, 152, 153
Steel. *See also* Blades
alloy. *See* Alloy steel
cutting of, with band saw, 64, 65
with torch, 63, 64
decarburization of, 106, 108
discoloration of, 106–8
drawing on, 61, 62
etching designs in, 211–31
grain growth and, 111
hardening of, quenching bath

and, 113–15
quenching temperature for, 111–13
hardness of, 106, 108–11
tempering and, 110
internal decay of, 106, 108
internal stress of, 110
kinds of, 14–16
for knifemaking, 254–66
qualities of, 254–66
quenching temperature of, 111–13
saw-blade, analysis of, 16
corrosion of, 17
toughness of, 106, 108–11
wear resistance of, 108–11
Straight bevel, 70, 73
Straightening, of blades, 67, 123–26
of bolster, 125, 126
Stress, internal, of steel, 110
Stropping, of blade edges, 191, 192
by hand, 196
Sulfur, as steel alloy, 254

Tang. *See also* Handles
fitting scales to, 157–60
full-, 2
Temperature, acid bath etching and, 221
critical, of steel, 109
quenching, steel hardening and, 111–13
Tempering, of blades, 116, 117
definition of, 105
regrinding after, 206, 207. *See also* Grinding
steel hardness and, 110
Tempering colors, 116, 117
Test, for hardness, 119, 120
Thermocouple, for electric kilns, 35
Thermostats, for electric kilns, 35
Thonging chisel, 237
Tooling fluid, use of, 140
Tools. *See also name of tool*
for etching, 212
for hand-sharpening, 192–96
for knifemaking, 19–38
relationship with, 204

small, 37
Torches, 20
for cutting steel, 63, 64
oxyacetylene, 20
Toughness, blade quality and, 12, 13
of steel, 106, 108–11
Tungsten, as steel alloy, 252, 253
Two-man saws, as knife blades, 15
Two-wheel band saws, 34

Utility knives, 53–55

Vanadium, as steel alloy, 253
Variable speed motors, 22, 23
Vegetable knives, 41–43
Voltage, of electric power, 23, 24

Warpage, of blades, 106, 107
Water-cooled belt grinder, 207–9
Water-cooled three-wheel sander, 207
Wax, use of, in etching blades, 211–13
Wear resistance, blade quality and, 12, 13
of steel, 108–11
Wheels, buffing, 183
cleaning of, 186
grinding. *See* Grinding wheels
work. *See* Work wheels
Whetstone, cleaning of, 192, 193
Wire gauge, 24, 25
Wiring, for electric power, 24, 25
Wood, for handles, 4, 151
milling of, 151, 152
Wood checks, healing of, 174
Wood filler, 174
Work rests, for belt sanders, 31
for grinders, 27
Work wheels, for belt grinders, 30, 31
for belt sanders, 30, 31
Workmanship, in knifemaking, 7, 8
Workshop, arrangement of, 37, 38
lights in, 38